A REASONED LOOK AT
ASIAN
RELIGIONS

A REASONED LOOK AT

ASIAN RELIGIONS

DAVID L. JOHNSON, Ph.D.

BETHANY HOUSE PUBLISHERS
MINNEAPOLIS, MINNESOTA 55438
A Division of Bethany Fellowship, Inc.

Published by Bethany House Publishers
A Division of Bethany Fellowship, Inc.
6820 Auto Club Road, Minneapolis, MN 55438

Printed in the United States of America

Library of Congress Cataloging in Publication Data

Johnson, David L.
   A reasoned look at Asian religions.

   Bibliography: p.
   Includes index.
   1. Asia—Religions. I. Title.
BL1032.J64   1985   291'.095   85-9180
ISBN 0-87123-798-9 (pbk.)

DAVID L. JOHNSON, who received his education at Augsburg College in Minneapolis and the University of Iowa, holds a Ph.D. in the history of religions. He is a student of Asian and Western philosophy and has been a frequent visitor to Asia for research purposes. He is Department Chairman and teaches in the Humanities division at Indiana State University.

TABLE OF CONTENTS

INTRODUCTION

The goal of this book is to make Asian religious thought comprehensible to those who may have little or no background in religious or philosophical studies. It is intended for anyone curious about Asian thinking and attitudes. The book, however, is not simply a theological history or a listing of various doctrines of faith. Instead, it is both analytic and critical.

This book is *analytic* because it presents as accurately as possible the structure of major Asian religions. It pinpoints key ideas of each faith and examines them in terms of how they make sense of life— how they provide a worldview or a philosophy of life. This approach will help the reader understand what these major traditions say about the human condition and the purpose of life.

This work is *critical* because it examines the ordering ideas of each religion in terms of their rational and moral limits. It asks the critical question, "What does it mean to hold to such doctrines and ideas?" Or "What results—mental and moral—are the logical consequences of holding to such beliefs?" Criticism, then, emerges from rational study of the logic of the faiths as well as from scrutiny of the philosophical soundness of their major claims. In other words, do their ideas hold together logically? Do their claims accurately describe reality? And what are the implications of holding to such ideas?

A critical position requires a frame of reference. My viewpoint is shaped by years of immersion within the Christian tradition of faith as well as a loyalty to a rationalist stance in religious and philosophical discussion.

Rationalism is somewhat out of fashion in the study of religion. Thinkers of a scientific (or positivist) persuasion view religion as irrelevant to debates about what is real and important in this world. Thinkers concerned about "self-realization" and "self-actualization" (Existentialists) think rational study of religion does not fit a discussion of religious issues. Both assert that religion deals not with reason but with an eruption into human life of the irrational, the pre-rational, the unconscious, or the pre-conscious. So they study religion as though it were an area of psychology.

Yet many statements made by believers are presented as truth claims, and the systems of belief are presented for general acceptance. Those statements must therefore be interpreted as claims, not as grist for a Freudian or Jungian mill of interpretation. Psychological methods always end up informing people they are not actually saying what they think they are saying. Religious claims are interpreted as psychological symptoms of deep inner and preconscious conditions of the human psyche. Indeed, maybe some are. But if believers put forward truth claims, then it is far more generous to treat those statements as such than to treat them as symptoms of irrational needs. On the other hand, the implications of holding a rationalist viewpoint are spelled out in the pages that follow.

Can a person with a Christian stance validly scrutinize another belief system? Many think that only someone irreligious or nonreligious can accurately describe another faith. Such a view is erroneous, because someone who holds a religious commitment can more easily identify what is religion and what is not. Moreover, such a person might be able to devise a method for study which assures a measure of objectivity. In short, religious sensitivity cuts two ways: it aids in understanding and it helps to avoid ruthless and inappropriate criticism.

Claiming that only a nonreligious person could write objectively might force one to discount the diagnostic skills of physicians who suffer illness of any sort; to discredit the writings of athletes who write about sports; and to look with suspicion upon studies of marriage written by married people. This, of course, would be a mistake.

In a work of this sort there are many who assist without knowing it. I owe much to the writing of Robert Baird, Karl Potter, William Christian, and Agehananda Bharati. University colleagues deserve thanks difficult to express in a few words. With Professors Donald Jennermann and Gary Foulk I spent many hours talking, arguing, debating, disagreeing. And they generously shared their books, ideas, and encouragement which helped me immeasurably. I am fortunate to work in a university department where ideals of integrity and excellence are held high by people of insight and good will.

To Indiana State University and to the J. Paul Leonard Library at San Francisco State University I owe a great deal. The former gave me time to write; the latter provided generous assistance in research.

A writer's acknowledgments often appear to be a mere token

recognition of those who endure the hardships of life with a writer. In this case, however, a written tribute seems not enough. Those who lived with me endured the silence and isolation necessary for the shuffling of words upon words and sentences upon sentences, which finally make a book. To Rebecca and Nicole, wife and daughter, I dedicate this work. It contains a good deal more of their kindness and understanding than they will ever know.

D. L. Johnson
San Francisco
1984

Chapter 1

EXPLORING THE ASIAN RELIGIONS

Exploring Asian religions is fearsome and troubling for many. Some even suspect that a close look at another faith might entail conversion to its claims. Some people worry that knowledge of another faith may weaken commitment to one's own. Many avoid any contact with other religions, content to cultivate isolation from rival faiths. They hope that ignoring complicated, and sometimes attractive ideas, will render them ineffective and invalid.

Such is not the case, however. And the numbers of spiritual nomads wandering many paths in search of enlightenment discredits the choice of ignorance. Other faiths remain; and they compel the curiosity, if not the steady allegiance, of many.

Moreover, it is increasingly difficult to maintain an isolated indifference to other faiths. Cultural and religious boundaries are fast breaking down. Muslim mosques are going up today in American cities large and small. Hindu temples dedicated to unfamiliar gods or goddesses appear in the most unlikely places and are frequented by surprising numbers of sophisticated devotees. The advantages of Oriental meditation techniques (to say nothing of martial arts) emerge on television screens in regular sequence with advertisements for automobiles, deodorants, and health club memberships. And hardly a college or university exists which does not offer courses exploring Oriental religions. The names of Asian mystics and teachers share space with political figures, movies stars, sportsmen, and commentators in the popular media.

A run-through of familiar names and movements shows the popularity of the Asian alternatives. These people have occasionally been tagged as hucksters of a superficial brand of meditation or mysticism. But they attract followers in sufficient numbers to make them notable.

One might begin with the Maharishi Mahesh Yogi. Many think

he laid the foundations for the tidal wave of interest in Asian meditation that hit the West in the 1960s. The Maharishi came to America
and Europe after completing a college degree in India, a thirteen-year
apprenticeship to a genuine Indian *swami*, and two years in a Hi-
malayan cave. He emerged with new ideas for meditation which he
termed Transcendental Meditation, a "practical, non-religious technique."

Many rich and famous, wearied by drug-induced euphoria, flocked
to the guru's meditation centers. Millions practiced this watered-
down version of a 2500-year-old Hindu discipline by sitting for a few
minutes a day and repeating mysterious *mantras* given them for a fee
by graduates of the Maharishi International University (now located
in Fairfield, Iowa). The Maharishi soon found himself at the head of
a multi-million dollar business which administered not only enlightenment for a fee but films, records, posters, and television appear-
ances.

Swami Satchidananda caught national attention during a popular
music festival called Woodstock. Sitting on a white bedspread among
the half-million music-mad youth, Satchidananda endorsed their quest
for peace and tranquillity. "Through music we can work wonders,"
he said. "Music is the celestial sound and it is sound that controls the
whole universe." Satchidananda settled himself in America to teach
access to "celestial sound" by opening the Integral Yoga Institute.
Devotees continue to study his form of meditation at the Satchidananda Ashram-Yogaville in Connecticut.

A. C. Bhaktivedanta Swami Prabhupada founded the International Society for Krishna Consciousness in 1966. He appeals to academics and youth alike. The "Hare Krishna" movement provides
not only respectable translations of traditional Hindu texts, but ceremonies and festivities complete with tamborines, chanting, and the
flinging of sugar at garish images of deities. In spite of sometimes
annoying and inappropriate conduct soliciting money for the movement, the shaven, robed devotees often demonstrate surprising education and polish when discussing their faith. Many of them even
learn to read Sanskrit.

Old Swami Prabhupada emphasized a small amount of learning
for his followers, but the younger Bhagwan Shree Rajneesh emphasizes ignorance. Rajneesh, before taking his vow of silence in the early
1980s, sang the praises of ignorance by rendering new meaning to
Socrates' confession that he did not know much, but that he was
wiser than others because he *knew* he did not know much. Rajneesh
advocates cultivating a simple, ignorant, spontaneous life. He himself

has managed to parlay the cultivation of ignorance into a fleet of Rolls Royces and a marvelously expensive lifestyle.

The list cannot end without mention of Guru Maharaj Ji, the pudgy Perfect Master of the Divine Light Mission. While still a young boy he inherited a respected religious institution in India and pro-claimed himself an *avatar* (incarnation) of God. By age thirteen he was in America spreading his teaching (transmitting "knowledge" by the touch of his hand). By age fifteen he had garnered enough follow-ers and cash to rent the Houston Astrodome for a three-day festival.

Eloquence, compassion, and an acute sensitivity to Asian thought mark the life of Alan Watts. He established credentials as a religious figure by taking ordination as an Episcopalian clergyman. Then he moved toward Zen Buddhism and published a thoroughly respectable book on Zen teaching. From there he took the role of providing pa-ternal guidance and common sense concerning mystical experience to millions of seekers who read his many books and listened to his radio broadcasts. The message he presented appears simplistic to the point of vacuousness. Yet many still think that Alan Watts' work bears the key to living well in a changing world: "Unless one is able to live fully in the present, the future is a hoax."

The pages that follow address the issues of contemporary Asian religions only indirectly. Our major concern is to accurately describe the fundamental assertions of major Asian traditions. For the most part, this requires looking at history and at major ideas. Such a task is analytic in the sense that we are searching for the fundamental ideas which provide a structure for faith.

But we will be critical as well as analytic. We will be critical in the sense that we will point out the margins of the particular tradi-tions—intellectual, social, and moral. The critical aspect of the book is somewhat out of fashion among academic historians of religions. Academics generally choose to suspend critical judgment when deal-ing with religions other than their own. This "suspension" of judg-ment follows from a real interest to discover what people of other faiths believe and what such believing entails. Critical judgment, it is thought, often gets in the way of understanding. Avoiding a dis-tortion of religious ideas at the same time as critically judging is such a problem that most scholars choose to abandon the critical task in favor of accurate description.

Thus the critical aspects of this book require some methodological foundations. The remainder of this chapter describes these founda-tions. Those readers who have no interest in such a problem (a prob-lem important mainly to scholars) may move ahead to the next chapter without feeling guilty and start reading about Confucianism.

METHODOLOGICAL ISSUES

Asian religions, even more than others, require the clarification of principles of study at the outset. We encounter three general problems when exploring Asian religions. The three problems might be labelled as Method, Definition, and Understanding.

Method is a persistent problem in religious studies, probably because of the nature of religion itself. In short, it raises the question of how to go about studying a religion which is not one's own in a fair and impartial manner. Is there a method of study which will grant understanding without distorting the facts?

The method issue is a difficult one. And there is no shortage of books that deal with it. The complicated nature of the issue is apparent; traditionally, religious study was done from within a particular religious group. One went to Sunday school or to Bible school or to seminary. But this study was of a similar sort: its aim was to establish a sense of the truth concerning the claims of the religion. In other words, the sort of study one ordinarily does when looking at religion is a normative study: the quest is for truth.

But when looking at another religious tradition, the first honest aim is to know the truth *about* that religion, not the truth *of* the religion. If I want to study Hinduism, I do not want to convert to Hinduism. I merely want to gain an accurate sense of what Hindus believe to be true. In short, I want to have the religion described to me. (I do not want to have it forced upon me as something to which I should give allegiance.)

There are two ways to study religion: normative study and descriptive study. The one searches for norms, for truths; the other, to understand. The distinction is worth keeping in mind. The primary goal of this book is to provide an accurate description of Asian religions by presenting fundamental ideas as a framework for faith. However, particular religious claims which fall short of consistency with other claims or claims leading to specific ethical or logical problems will be noted.

This study, then, is both analytic and critical. It is analytic in the sense that we will give data concerning fundamental doctrines and beliefs. It is critical in the sense that some ideas are appraised in terms of their logical and ethical implications. Readers, of course, are free to judge the accuracy of the analysis and the validity of the critique. More specific statements about the nature of religious truth claims follow the discussion of the problem of Understanding.

The problem of Definition is related to the Method issue. What is meant by the word "religion" needs clarification. A look at Asian traditions suggests that their religions are extremely different from religions in the West. Many of the Asian religions ignore the question of whether or not God exists. Often they do not speak to the moral issues familiar to Christians or Jews. And often they seem to have a reduced concern for individual persons but an inflated concern for family, caste, or society.

In short, how must one define religion in order to be able to include the Asian traditions under the category of religion? Moreover, how does one define religion so that the religious dimension of life gets marked off from other concerns and activities of life? Clearly, it will not do to define religion as "belief in God." That would eliminate from consideration most of the faiths of Asia. We must find a general definition for the word "religion" which will allow us to consider all sorts of religions, not just one. Finding a general definition is complicated by the fact that much of what is included under the word "religion" in Asian societies is not what is included under the word in Western societies. For example, Muslims do not easily distinguish between claims concerning religious life and those of political life. Muslim scripture does not admit a distinction between the rule of God in individual lives and in the political sphere. How, then, can religion be defined so that a Muslim's concerns about the social and political order will be recognized as "religious" concerns?

Some requirements for a general definition can be stated:

1. A general definition should be broad enough to cover many (even all) instances of religion.
2. A general definition should be narrow enough to limit the use of the word to specific aspects of life (i.e., to distinguish between what is religious and what is recreation, work, politics, etc.).
3. A general definition should be neutral with regard to the truth question (the definition must not by itself imply that some faiths are false).
4. A general definition should be stipulative and functional. That is, the definition must be an analytic category (not necessarily an empirical category), and it must be usable, workable, for purposes of analytic clarity.

A general definition, then, provides an unbiased, neutral category under which various religions might be ranged. The need for the four requirements listed is apparent if we look at current definitions of religions. One that has considerable acceptance today is Freud's psychological definition of religion. He presented it as a general definition. Yet it fails to meet the requirements stipulated, and, in fact, functions as a religious proposal (or an anti-religious proposal). Freud's definition, roughly stated, is that "religion is a wish-dream which enables people to accept the terrors and injustices of human life." That is, people construct religions because of a psychological need to compensate for the fact that life is often unfair and cruel. In Freud's view, religion is a neurosis; it is a crutch for weak minds. Such a general definition is clearly inadequate for an unbiased, descriptive study of religion.

Another definition holding some currency today is Sir James Frazer's definition presented in his tome *The Golden Bough: A Study in Comparative Religion*. Frazer holds that primitives turn first to magic to solve their problems. Then when magic fails they invent religion. Finally, as people grow to intellectual sophistication, they discover the method of science as a way to deal with life's problems. Religion, then, is an organized effort to solve problems by intellectually obsolete means. Religion has been replaced by science as a way to solve problems in the same way that religion displaced magic.

Again, the definition of religion must be checked against the requirements for a general definition. It fails. To consider religion a sophisticated form of magic or a naive science prejudges the truth and worth of religion prior to an encounter with any specific religion. Thus, Frazer's definition is not neutral with regard to the truth question, and it is unlikely that it is broad enough to include those faiths which have no interest in social, political, or environmental problem-solving.

A FUNCTIONAL DEFINITION OF RELIGION

For a definition to be a general definition, it must distinguish religion from other concerns and activities of life. And it must not by itself be some sort of religious proposal (i.e., it must not be a statement put forward for acceptance by people).

We *can* construct a general definition useful for the study of Asian religions. One successful definition is that religion is the condition of being "ultimately concerned."

This definition can be traced to the theologian Paul Tillich. He used the phrase to point out the nature of faith—faith is not simply believing in something for which there is a low degree of evidence, nor is it simply a discipline of the will. Faith, he maintained, is to feel grasped by something which concerns one ultimately.

Though Tillich was a theologian and concerned to make Christian faith the basis for his constructive system of theology, the definition of religion as ultimate concern can be used as a broad general definition (if Tillich's specific theological content is put aside). Religion as *ultimate concern* can be a general descriptive definition of what it means for a person to be religious.

What is meant by ultimate concern is that people, while they have many concerns in life (food, clothing, shelter, sex, together with cognitive and aesthetic concerns), find that occasionally a concern claims ultimacy. If a concern claims ultimacy it demands total surrender. A concern becomes ultimate when it is felt to make an unconditional demand.

An ultimate concern also promises complete fulfillment at the same time as it makes a demand. Both demand and promise are combined in an ultimate concern. The nature of fulfillment is not always precisely stated. It may be expressed in indefinite and unspecific symbols. Within the Asian traditions such words as *nirvana, moksha, sukhavati,* and *satori* are used to express the goal of fulfillment. Someone who surrenders to the demand of the concern believes that complete fulfillment follows.

This general definition is helpful because it does not define what is of ultimate concern. That is, the definition is not a religious proposal. It simply states that some people do have concerns which claim ultimacy for them. It does not say which concerns *ought* to claim ultimacy. Moreover, the definition is broad enough to include many claims of what might be of ultimate concern—Buddhist, Hindu, Taoist, Confucian, Muslim. Each religion identifies its own concern as ultimate (and they disagree with one another). But the definition is saying only that each has a concern which it claims to be *ultimate.* Finally, the definition is narrow enough so that not all concerns of people need be studied. Only ultimate concerns are to be studied.

So then, to define religion as that which concerns people ultimately means that there are people in the world who experience some concern for which they feel the need to make a complete surrender. In doing so, they believe they are doing what will bring final fulfillment. Therefore religion should not be thought of simply as a discipline or a crutch or an opiate or a superstition. Some people elevate to a level of ultimacy things which are in fact not ultimate. For example, some totally surrender themselves to money, to fame, to success or to popularity. Some elevate to ultimacy social revolution, liberty, equality, "self-realization" or "self-actualization." Any of these vagaries might be elevated to ultimacy. When they are elevated to such a place by people, someone may want to study them as religions. But the major value of the definition is this. It provides a neutral category which arranges religious ideas and claims so that the structure of a faith is made clear without immediately judging the faith as right or wrong, good or bad, true or false. Analysis of the truth value of any specific claim is done only after it has been established as a "religious" claim. The definition helps to make clear what sorts of claims are religious. And it assists in making clear the important distinction between whether or not a claim is a religious truth claim or actually true. The distinction is important because a person needs first to find what are in fact the truth claims of a religion. Then one might want to determine whether or not the claims are true or false. To confuse the two issues leads to great misunderstanding. This definition of religion helps to avoid such problems by providing a neutral definition under which to arrange various claims.

THE PROBLEM OF UNDERSTANDING

A third problem follows. Is it possible to understand a religion other than one's own?

People of Asian traditions often contend that it is impossible for a Westerner to grasp the ideas of the East. There is a superficial soundness to such a claim. It is true that insiders and outsiders have access to different data. And there is, to be sure, something about a religious commitment which a nonreligious observer will never comprehend. But all sorts of human experiences have a private, inner, unique dimension. It is one thing to study the history of women's liberation movements. It is another to live with a liberated woman as spouse. It is one thing to study the history of warfare. It is another to be an infantryman under fire. The point granted is that there are levels of understanding. And it might be the case that a student of religions will never comprehend in the sense of a mind committed to a particular religion.

However, it is important to consider what information is available to the observer. Available data generates a considerable understanding of religions. There are written histories of religions. There are theological and philosophical texts which emerge from some faiths. And believers produce creative works of art and literature. Often there is an incredible amount of material available to anyone who wants to make a concentrated study of a particular religion.

But attention needs to be given to how people communicate ultimate concerns. There are two basic modes of communication: (1) indirect and implicit; (2) direct and explicit. The implicit mode of communication is an insider's language that relies heavily upon symbols, stories, and rituals shared with other believers. The explicit mode of communication is the mode used to consciously clarify ideas held by a religious group and to express those ideas to outsiders.

Let us give some attention to the two modes. The implicit mode makes use of symbols, stories, and rituals. These may originate at a preconscious level of experience. They are unspecific in meaning and open to varied interpretations. To understand symbol, story, and ritual requires close attention to how the believers in question understand them. That might require observing them, reading some of their books, or asking them specific questions.

What symbols, stories, and rituals do is a matter to note as well. Symbols are often confused with signs, but they differ in function. Signs point to something beyond themselves; symbols *participate* at the same time as they point. A symbol carries with it something of that to which it points. For instance, a nation's flag is more than a sign of a nation; it is a symbol of a nation itself. The symbol *participates* in what it points to.

Another characteristic of a symbol is that for a believer, it opens, or reveals, some meaning not revealed to a nonbeliever. What makes it a symbol for people is this strange power to communicate to some and not to others. A third characteristic is that a symbol is not produced intentionally. And fourth, a symbol seems to possess a life of its own—it rises into the conscious lives of people, but it also fades and dies. Tracing the rise and fall of symbols among religious people is a preoccupation of many religious historians.

Stories, however, are another way religious ideas are passed along. Symbols never appear in isolation; they are always tied together by some story. The stories are sometimes of historical interest; they tie themselves to some incident or event. But believers generally are not concerned about the historical aspects of the story. The *message* is important.

Within religions there are various kinds of stories which might be identified. There are stories of origins, stories that tell who people are and why they are in the world. There are stories that provide exemplary patterns of behavior, such as, What is the proper thing to do when a father dies? And there are stories which help to explain troubling events, reasons for a disease which decimated a neighboring village, for example. Such stories arrange symbols in such a way that they speak comfort or insight or encouragement to people in various situations. And while the stories continue to speak to believers, they continue to be passed along.

Finally, the implicit mode of communication also makes use of rituals. Rituals dramatize stories. And because the stories are dramatized, a believer is able to participate in what is of ultimate concern, what is really most important in the world. A ritual does two things. First, by reenacting a story, the time of the sacred event is made present for the believer. A believer is then able to reenact a period of time he considers to be holy. Second, a ritual empowers or transforms a person into something he was not before he performed the ritual. A ritual then, is thought by the believer to be something that changes him, that makes him whole, or new, or powerful.

Symbols, stories, rituals seem to emerge out of a preconscious, even preliterate, condition. They are most easily studied among primitive peoples where no conscious and critical reflection has been done concerning the symbols or stories. Once critical reflection occurs, a new mode of communication develops.

The explicit mode employs doctrine, dogma, and the written word. Doctrine specifically states the ideas of the faith, usually in propositional form. Doctrine's intent is to articulate as clearly as possible that which is of ultimate concern. Moreover, doctrine also spells out the regulations or norms of faith and worship. Doctrine also is employed to define and defend the faith in relation to other faiths.

Dogma appears in a religion only when it is organized in a unified, hierarchical manner. Dogma appears when there is a recognized, official religious authority. That is because dogma is an authoritative resolution of a doctrinal disagreement. It is intended to provide greater clarity and precision in statements of faith. Once a dogmatic decision has been made, any who continue to assert their own private opinions on the matter are eliminated from the ranks of the faithful.

Sacred writings include scriptures and other writings considered important by a group sharing faith. Generally, scriptural writings are thought to be revealed in some special way. What constitutes "revelation," however, is a matter of some disagreement among religious groups. Hindus hold that their scripture is what was "heard" (shruti) by ancient sages. Muslims hold that their scripture was "dictated" to Muhammad by an angel and that it corresponds exactly to an original book residing in heaven with Allah.

The authority given to scripture is a matter that any student of religion must determine by study of the text and the commentaries written about the text. Commentaries and the writings of great and respected leaders often carry an importance very close to the sacred words of a scripture. In Hinduism the text called *Bhagavad Gita* is not technically scripture, but it ranks so high that most modern Hindus prefer to quote from it when discussing their faith. For Muslims the *Hadith*, traditions associated with Muhammad and his companions, ranks very high as a chief means by which to interpret the scripture.

Attention to the ways in which religions are communicated aids understanding. This requires sensitivity to symbols and rituals, even if at first they seem strange and offensive. It is important to see how symbols and rituals fit into a larger pattern of beliefs which constitute a worldview. This text will not concentrate upon symbols or rituals, however. And stories will appear only where they enhance description or explanation of doctrines. Primary attention is given to explicit assertions. Our effort is to show how religions provide a system of belief and values.

Critical work concerning the Asian religions is done with some care. Systems of beliefs are of more concern than specific claims made by Asian religions. Critical attention will often be given to the systems rather than to specific claims. This means that questions concerning whether or not rebirth actually occurs, whether Karma is the case, or whether Muhammad really spoke with an angel are not seen as the most important issues to be addressed. Rather, we will give attention to how such claims fit into a larger pattern of belief.

Let us remember that not all religious statements are truth claims. Some are expressive statements, some injunctive, some declarative, some evocative. This means that not all claims are being put forward for acceptance by advocates of a particular religion. The distinction is worth noting, if only to help to avoid long, tedious arguments over issues which cannot be resolved by rational means.

Some characteristics of truth claims can be stated. First, a truth claim is capable of consistent formulation in more than one way (evocative and expressive statements often are not). Second, a truth claim is a claim liable to significant disagreement. It is presented as a statement that makes a difference if one holds to it. Third, a truth claim permits some reference to its logical subject (what a statement refers to). Fourth, a truth claim must be a statement for which it is possible to give some support. It must have some sort of evidence which might count for or against it.

Many religious claims simply do not fit requirements for truth claims. Thus, attention to the larger system of belief serves as the best way to exercise some critical judgment concerning a religion. The exploration of Asian religions offers an opportunity to grapple with fascinating ideas and to assess proposals for belief critically.

RECOMMENDED READING

Baird, Robert D. *Category Formation and the History of Religions.* Mouton, 1971.

Christian, William. *Meaning and Truth in Religion.* Princeton University Press, 1964.

Smart, Ninian. *Worldviews. Crosscultural Explorations of Human Beliefs.* Charles Scribner's Sons, 1983.

Streng, Frederick. *Understanding Religious Life.* Dickenson Publishing Co., 1976.

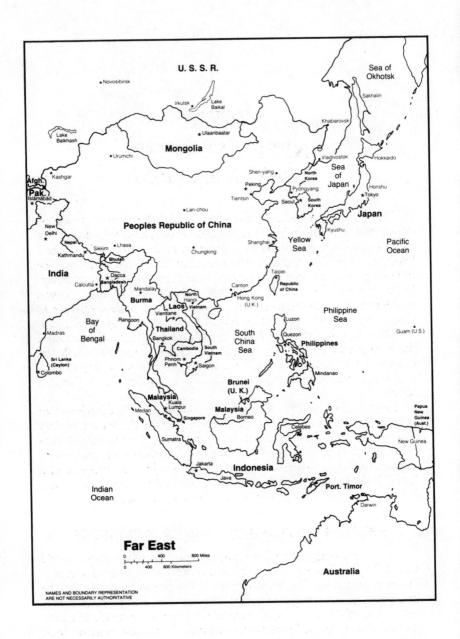

Far East

Chapter 2

CHINESE RELIGIONS— CONFUCIANISM

China has produced religious ideas quite different from India. So different in fact that when Buddhism entered China from India, the Chinese government condemned the religion as barbaric. China had lived for some time with Confucianism as an official religion. The state allowed a number of unofficial religions to exist alongside Confucianism; the chief among them was Taoism. But officials viewed Buddhism as a troublesome faith because of its origins outside of China and because a foreign faith might pose a threat to social order.

Their hostile attitude toward Buddhism is but one indication of the strength of an entirely unique religious orientation which the Chinese held. To survive in China, Buddhism had to modify its doctrines and practices enough to make them compatible to Chinese tastes.

From an early period, China had possessed an official religion of refined gentility and elaborate ceremony maintained not by a priestly class but by an official scholar class. Foundations for the formal state religion rested upon distinctly Chinese presuppositions concerning the nature of the universe, the nature of human life, and proper moral living. From such presuppositions and in a context of unique historical events, a particular range of religious options emerged.

PRESUPPOSITIONS OF CHINESE RELIGIONS

From very early times the Chinese assumed views of the world that differ significantly from the thinkers of India or the thinkers of Western societies. The first of these is the presupposition that the universe originated by some natural process. The presupposition does not necessarily deny the existence of God or the existence of supernatural forces, but it holds that some natural process must account for the origin of things. In fact, the issue of origin is never of much concern to Chinese thinkers.

Yet the disinterest in the question of how and when things began probably arises from a distinct view of the nature of the universe itself. They believed that the universe is a self-contained and self-operating whole. The world requires no outside, external force either to get it going or to maintain its operations. The universe is to be explained in terms of itself, its own ways of operating, and its own powers or forces.

Even the most important deity mentioned in Chinese mythology (T'ien) is often translated into English simply as the word "heaven." And though T'ien is sometimes mentioned in a context where he (or it) shows some capacity to exercise control over nature and human events, he (or it) is never described as a Creator, nor are any specific human characteristics assigned. And many times the word T'ien is used simply to name the sky. With the rise of various schools of philosophical speculation, all suggestions of a divinity were eliminated.

A second presupposition is that the process of change is cyclical. The world is constantly changing, but it changes according to a fixed pattern which is circular. The model used to illustrate such change is the change of seasons. Spring, summer, fall and winter occur in a regular sequence, year after year, without altering their cyclical pattern.

The presupposition concerning cyclical change is important because it encourages Chinese thinkers to consider all change as relative change. No change is final, complete, or absolute. Nothing ever stays the same, but the change taking place is always part of a process of return to what was reality earlier in the cycle. The changes of winter mean that eventually summer will appear again. Winter, then, is relative to summer.

Thus all change takes place by everything moving toward its opposite and then back to itself again. Human beings ought to be aware of the way that change occurs. The wise man orders his affairs to coincide with the cyclical process.

A third presupposition reinforces the notion of cyclical change. The pattern of human history follows the same cyclical pattern found in nature. Even as nature goes through changes of a regular sequence—summer, fall, winter and spring—so do human events, bringing about a return to what was the case earlier. In fact, early Chinese historians searched for reasons to associate specific periods of history with specific calendar seasons and their sequence. If one king's rule was seen to correspond to winter, it should be expected that his successor's rule would correspond to spring. As spring differs from winter, so would the rule of the "spring" king differ in policies, procedures, and programs from the "winter" king.

Thus it is presupposed that human affairs and natural phenomena are closely linked and interrelated. In fact, the relationship between human life and nature is considered to be an organic relationship, not a mechanical one. What takes place in the natural world corresponds to events in the world of human affairs. Just as the human body as an organic whole responds at some distant place when it is stressed at a near place (e.g. when you reach forward to lift a heavy object, your back—a distant part of the body—responds), so human affairs adjust when nature does something. And when human beings do things, nature responds to what is done. Nature may exhibit stress because of human acts. Or it may reflect a balance and harmony with human acts.

The central concern of religious thought in China follows from these presuppositions concerning man and nature. That concern is to bring about and to maintain harmony: the order of human life is to be structured in such a way as to correspond to the order of the universe. Religious thought, then, has serious social-political implications for Chinese thinkers. The sage must spell out the necessary conditions for the establishment and maintenance of cosmic order; he must show how mankind can be ruled so that harmony prevails.

These presuppositions tend to make Chinese religious thought very pragmatic. The test of truth for the sage is whether or not what he says works. Does what he says bring about harmony among mankind and with nature? Ideas must work in practice. Even when Mao Tse Tung took leadership of China with his special interpretation of revolutionary Marxism, this principle prevailed (although Mao avoided the label pragmatist). Mao rejected ideological and theoretical speculation which did not directly apply to social conditions. The Cultural Revolution of the 1960s saw intellectuals thrown out of their university positions and put to work in factories and farms. Mao's purpose was to show scholar and peasant alike that if ideas have no practical value, they are of no use to anyone. In at least one way ancient Chinese presuppositions survived even Mao's Marxist revolution.

A unique social structure for traditional China followed from the presuppositions. China assumed that a king must rule. The king was considered to be the "Son of Heaven." He ruled by the permission of heaven, known as "Mandate of Heaven." The king's advisors, too, were of crucial importance (they assured that he abided by the requirements of the Mandate). So important were the advisors that an educational system was instituted to identify and to train the brightest and most capable people to serve as government functionaries. An examination system led the brightest students all the way to the highest administrative positions of the government. This scholar class was elevated to a position of social and political prestige just under the king-emperor. The task of the scholar-officials was to order human affairs so as to maintain a balance with the natural world. Scholars advised the king on how to act, when to act, and with what measures to act so as to assure harmony.

Beneath the scholar-officials in status were the landowners. This class's wealth was tied to the workings of nature, the natural order. They supported the scholar class with their income and exploited knowledge to assure that their actions, too, were orderly.

Beneath the landowners were merchants, skilled artisans, and, of course, peasants. Peasants worked the land as tenant farmers and laborers. Artisans contributed their skills to building and maintaining necessary tools and equipment for an efficient agricultural economy. And business people engaged in trading. Businessmen were somewhat suspect as a group because they were removed from direct concern with the natural order. In fact, they gained their advantage and wealth by exploiting the products of nature at the marketplace. (They use what is produced in nature to create their wealth.) And though they had an important and necessary function in society, the function was looked upon as less worthy than either farming the land or studying.

Finally, at the very bottom of the social heap was the military—both soldiers and officers of law. Their lives were controlled by the disciplines of combat and violence. Though one task of theirs was to maintain peace, they were generally preoccupied with disharmony and a disruption of order. Efforts to temper military tendencies toward disorder resulted in strategies of warfare that were largely defensive and often passive.

The social system following from the presuppositions is not a caste system. It is merely a social hierarchy reflecting the values that flow out of the presuppositions. And, of course, the social structure is theoretical. In practice, as might be expected, great importance was attached to the military. And no nation survives long without a strong class of business people skilled in commercial enterprise. Nevertheless, at least in official theory, scholars were highly regarded and military people denigrated within the social system.

With the success of Confucius' teaching (as early as the second century B.C.) the rough outlines of a stratified society appeared. And the thinking associated with this stratification endured for centuries.

CONFUCIUS AND THE PHILOSOPHERS OF ORDER

The teachings of Confucius have been an inseparable part of Chinese society and thought since the time of the Han Dynasty (from ca. 206 B.C.). The texts upon which the teaching is based (the Confucian Classics) are not the collection of a particular sect but the literary heritage of a whole people and culture.

Confucius is the Latinized form of the Chinese K'ung Fu Tzu. He lived from roughly 551 to 479 B.C., during the decline of the third great Chinese dynasty, the Chou (pronounced "Joe").

The Chou Dynasty dates from about 1050 B.C. when the Chou nobles overthrew the Shang Dynasty rulers. They justified their revolt on the principle that proper order and harmony was not being maintained. Thus, heaven demanded that a new ruler accept the Mandate and restore order to the world. After the revolt, the Chou rulers parcelled out the territories according to a feudal system called the "well-field." The well-field was a system of dividing land into sections of nine squares, with the owner of each section of land occupying the central square. The owner granted various of the remaining eight squares to others in exchange for a percentage of the farm products grown on the land. The owner promised protection and certain administrative services to his tenants.

The well-field system worked nicely for a time (i.e., for the first few generations of owners and tenants). Power and wealth were measured by land holdings because agriculture was the basis of the Chou Dynasty economy. Moreover, the social system was held together by the sense of reciprocal obligation between tenant and landowner. The one was obligated to work the land productively and serve the landlord. The other was obligated to maintain order by means of overseeing the extended territory, ordering relations among various tenants, and offering some administrative and judicial support. The landowning families retained scholars as official experts in understanding the affairs of mankind and knowledge of how things are to be done properly to assure order and success. Confucius was one of these scholars retained by nobility to provide expert advice.

Yet Confucius was somewhat itinerant in his professional life. He never stayed long with any one family or prince that he advised. He attracted a following of students during his travels from household to household, and they recorded his sayings and passed them along.

And though Confucius died in obscurity, his ideas continued after him.

THE SOCIAL CONTEXT OF CONFUCIUS' THOUGHT

When the Chou government collapsed, various teachers rose who claimed to know how to restore order. The collapse was no sudden happening, but a gradual disintegration. It was chronicled by historians who spared few details in describing the horrors of a society torn by civil strife. Two factors contributed significantly toward the collapse of the social order. One was the direct fault of the feudal economy of early China. Land ownership was the key to wealth and power within Chou society. It was the most important commodity, the major medium of exchange (farm products were exchanged, but they came from the land), and it was the basis for wealth. But the wealth of land was tied to the land's ability to produce necessary crops. Such a situation required that each major household maintain a standing army to protect land from encroachment by other greedy landlords wishing to expand their power and wealth.

Thus, military life became a necessary preoccupation of the noble families. The art of warfare, the myth of strength, the strategies of defense and attack became requirements for survival. Historical evidence indicates that warfare became widespread for long periods of time as nobles fought one another to increase their wealth. By the late 8th century B.C. (long before Confucius was even born), the Chou family rulers were little more than puppets in the hands of their most powerful vassals to whom Chou's ancestors had given land. As a result, China was left without any centralized authority or government which could exercise control over an extended territory. China became one vast battleground, with each noble taking what he could get.

A second factor in the decline of the Chou rule was a movement away from agricultural life. As the population gradually shifted toward the river areas of north China, agriculture's dominance waned. The business and trading class began to take on increased significance. The rise of a new intermediary class dealing with the exchange of goods meant that the old economic system based upon land ownership and agriculture was threatened as the merchant class began to rise.

One result of the rise of a merchant class to prominence was the loosening of the old relationships that lay at the heart of political and social life. The older system worked, to the extent that it did work, by the sense of reciprocal relations and obligations between landlord and tenant. Each held obligations toward the other. But merchants and tradesmen held no obligations within the older framework. Merchants were free entrepreneurs. They could deal with whomever they wished so long as the prices paid for goods and services were acceptable. The rise of a new class which held no place in the web of established reciprocal relations forced significant change. But the change threatened the stability and order of the whole society.

Confucius' thought developed out of this situation of change and disorder marked by warfare and collapsing relations between social classes. The important question facing Confucius and the society of his time was, "How can mankind live together in peace and order?" "How can harmony be established and maintained?"

In the most general sense Confucius' answer to the question is that society is held together by moral relationships which worked in an earlier time. According to Confucius, the time of the ancient dynasties (the Hsia, the Shang, and the early Chou) was a time of order and harmony, it was a Golden Age. The most significant characteristic of this age was an orderly relation among people. Moral relations, not wealth, made them exemplary and great. Moreover, the Golden Age can be rediscovered by careful study of the great books passed along from that time, the Classics. The Classical books were five: *The Book of Poetry, The Book of History, The Annals of Spring and Autumn, The Book of Rites,* and *The Book of Change.* These books, Confucius maintained, laid out the fundamental principles of order.

THE RIVAL VIEWS

The teaching of Confucius is difficult to isolate in any pure form. Complicated historical tradition surrounds the core of his thought as we receive it today. To unravel centuries of controversies, interpretations, and applications of his sayings to find the kernel of the master's teaching is impossible. Yet a body of assertions does survive which presents a view distinct from other specific views of the time.

It is important to remember that Confucian teaching emerges out of social and political chaos. And in any situation of disorder, there are stock answers as to how disorder might be ended and order restored. China developed classic answers which endure among social thinkers to this day, though today we find them clothed in vocabularies of somewhat greater sophistication than in Confucius' time. Ancient Chinese thinkers discussed issues posed yet today concerning order in the world.

One school of thought responding to the Chinese situation is called the Legalist School by some, the Realist School by others. Both names characterize the solution to the social anarchy of ancient China (or any other society, for that matter). The Realists give a simple answer to the question of how to make people behave: "Lay down the rules. And if people don't obey the rules, punish them!"

This view presents itself as realist in its assessment of human nature. It insists that the starting point of social thought must be with the fact that people are lazy, selfish, dishonest, and greedy. Any who set out to develop a theory of social order must begin at this realistic appraisal of human beings. Since people are lazy, selfish, dishonest, and greedy, it is necessary to build the social system upon such facts. Building upon the facts can be done in such a way as to put human vices to work for social order.

Realists advocated the principle of punishment and reward for controlling people. Everyone hates the pain of punishment, and everyone wants to be rewarded. The state, then, must be so organized that people are enticed to do what is right (by reward) and terrorized at the mere thought of doing what is wrong (punishment). Laws must promise punishment to those who disobey and reward to those who obey. The system must be elaborate in the sense that it provides a detailed description of acts which are permissible and acts which are not. And the state must have means by which it can mete out immediate and impartial punishment or reward. In short, this requires a police state of absolute authority which does exactly what is required by the law. The state apparatus must provide that each official live under the same rigid principles of punishment and reward as do ordinary citizens. Thus, order from the top to the bottom is assured. Laws as external requirements and duties for each individual provide a structure for order in society.

The famous names associated with the Realist School of ancient China are Li Ssu and Han Fei Tzu. These men's programs of social control make the work of Hitler and Stalin seem like the tentative and incomplete musings of amateurs. Nevertheless, the solutions of a Hitler or a Stalin to problems of social order are based upon similar assumptions. Some leaders in contemporary China look with favor on the social analysis of these ancient thinkers. Han Fei Tzu went so far as to say that, "If virtuous officials are employed by the prince, the people will love their own relations; but if wicked officials are employed, the people will love the law." That is to say, it is law which holds a society together, not love. Officials must act in such ways that citizens cling to the letter of the law for protection. Only law serves as a foundation for an orderly society.

Take a boy who is a bad character. His parents may get angry with him; he does not change. His neighbors may reprove him; it does not have any effect on him. His teachers may moralize to him; but he does not conform. All the excellent devices of which love of parents, conduct of neighbors, and wisdom of teachers may dispose are applied to him, but they remain totally without avail, and not a hair of his shins will change. But when the district official sends his soldiers and in the name of law searches for wicked individuals, then he becomes afraid, changes his principles, and reforms his conduct. So love of parents is not sufficient to teach a son morality, but the severe punishments of the officials are needed. People become naturally spoiled by love, but obedient to severity.[1]

Laws that demand uniform behavior, coupled with a ruthlessly exact application of punishment and reward, do wonders for making people live orderly lives, the Legalist-Realists maintained.

Against this hard-nosed assessment of human beings and its severe measures, quite a different school of thought appeared in ancient China. This was the school of Mo Ti (pronounced Moe Dee). The solution to social chaos was not force but love, Mo Ti insisted. The state ought to administer brotherly kindness and good will toward all, an all-embracing love. Then order will follow, for all people will act toward all other people in peace.

It is to regard the state of others as one's own, the persons of others as one's own self. . . . When all the people in the world love one another, then the strong will not overpower the weak, the many will not oppress the few, the wealthy will not mock the poor, the honored will not disdain the humble, and the cunning will not deceive the simple. And it is all due to mutual love that calamities, strifes, complaints, and hatred are prevented from arising.[2]

Mo Ti held that people must learn to demonstrate good will toward other people. Mo was not concerned about emotion or sentiment. Instead, he advocated the view that individuals and government need merely to structure behavior in such a way that people will be benefitted rather than injured by things that are done. Such a structuring of behavior need not be done for any altruistic or idealistic reasons, but simply for reasons of self-interest.

In a curious argument, Mo writes that all admit that the troubles of society result from hatred, jealousy, envy, and the favoring of one group or family over another group or family. Since troubles arise from these conditions, and since all would prefer that troubles did

[1]Han Fei Tzu
[2]Mo Ti

not occur, then the solution is simply to change behavior. Instead of hating and doing nasty things, people should love and do beneficial things to others. People will respond in the same way (if you give a man a gift, he will give a gift back; if you hit a man, he will hit you back). Instead of favoring some and disfavoring others when express, ing good will, people should act with concern for the welfare of all. In this way, people avoid the causes of social unrest and disorder, and all people end up benefitting. If the government adopts this policy, all get what they really want and the state abides in peace and order.

Mo's argument is patently utilitarian. He asks, "What do we really want in society? Do we want order? Do we want harmony?" If so, then we must do those things which bring order.

All actions can be judged in terms of their consequences. We need simply ask ourselves, "Does a particular policy bring benefit to people? Or does it benefit some while harming others?" Only what works to the benefit of all brings order. Thus discrimination is wrong because it results in resentment, envy, even injury to some. And disorder follows. However, everyone gets order if policies are set up so that all benefit. The government can order itself so that each gets what he wants. And, above all, each wants order, since nothing else comes his way unless there is order.

Thus Mo advocates a simple philosophy that holds to a utilitarian standard of assessing what is good and bad. If something works, if it brings desirable consequences, it is good. If something brings unde, sirable consequences, it is bad. No one needs to sit around pondering the nature of "good" or "bad." Good is what benefits. Bad is what harms. Even the most simple-minded knows that.

However, Confucius opposed both Realists and the followers of Mo Ti for specific reasons. He thought the Realists were superficial in their diagnosis and cure for social disorder. In short, he held that morality cannot completely be legislated. A government may lay down laws which prohibit theft, assault, deception and wickedness. But laws cannot make people friendly, courteous, respectful and kind. Laws cannot make any man into a "gentleman." Friendliness, cour, tesy, respect, generosity, magnanimity are the virtues of a gentleman. They are the moral requisites for good order and harmony. But laws cannot produce such qualities.

Confucius maintained that Mo Ti held a simplistic, even degen, erate, proposal for ordering human society. Mo Ti's ideas would re, duce humanity to the level of animals, Confucius maintained, because it bases moral behavior upon assumptions of profit and usefulness. Mo argued that the state's job is to induce people to act nicely by appealing to their selfishness. The state should convince people that it is in their own self-interest to act with concern for others. Yet such a view of moral behavior, Confucius argued, is subhuman. To appeal to self-interest as a motive for good behavior is to reduce morality to animal-training. Indeed, one might teach a dog to wag its tail, shake hands, roll over or exhibit courteous, even respectful, behavior. But the dog does what it does in order to get a reward (and to avoid punishment). The dog's acts are motivated by self-interest. Is that morality? Confucius asked. Are humans to be reduced to the level of animals to get them to act appropriately? Confucius was convinced that morality was something more than useful or profitable activity.

THE MORAL DIMENSION OF LIFE

The Confucian teaching concerning morality is encased in numerous aphorisms, anecdotes, and brief stories passed along in the text, *Analects*. The sayings at first appear to be pithy remarks more suitable for a collection of epigrams than for a religious text. Yet encased in the short statements is a specific view of the nature of morality and of "manhood at its best."

Confucius was concerned to discover that aspect of the human being which makes it unique, special. He wanted to show how that unique human quality might be expanded and developed to its fullest. The secret for harmony and order within human society lies in the development of the human dimension, he thought. Human beings must learn to express their unique nature in order to live proper and fulfilled lives.

Many of the writings passed along contain statements which concentrate upon the quality of righteousness, or goodness, or obligation, or duty. The Chinese word having these many meanings in English is *yi*.

A gentleman takes as much trouble to discover what is right (*yi*) as a lesser man takes to discover what will pay.
The noble-minded man comprehends righteousness (*yi*), the low-minded man comprehends profit.

The essential element in *yi* is the inner sense of obligation. People sense obligation in many different ways—obligation to work, to save, to dress appropriately, to eat proper foods. Confucius noted that people have a specific sense of obligation which is *unlike* the obligations which carry with them some beneficial consequence.

People feel obliged to eat well so that they will maintain their health. But such an obligation is a utilitarian obligation. A person acts under this sense of obligation in order to get something he wants—good health.

Confucius believed that humans possess a sense of obligation which is unaffected by possible results or consequences. Such an obligation is unconditional, absolute, without interest in profit or advantage. That is, a person feels obliged to do some acts simply for the sake of doing them. This sense of unconditional obligation to act in certain ways at certain times is the moral realm, Confucius maintained. A moral act is done for itself, for its own sake, for the doing of it, and not for any consequence it might bring. Thus the moral act is done unconditionally. And the moral value of the act lies in doing the act, not in any result which might come from doing the act.

Confucius believed that human beings are unique among the creatures of the world because they have an inner sense of unconditional obligation. Animals act always for the sake of some result. That is why a dog can be trained to behave in certain ways. Animals do things only because they are aware of punishments or rewards as consequences of acts. But human beings hold an inner sense of obligation to do some things simply for the sake of doing them. This is the moral realm, said Confucius.

The distinction Confucius wishes to make is crucial. He insists that someone who helps old ladies to cross a busy street because he wants to win a Boy Scout merit badge is not acting from morality. He is acting for profit. Confucius is insisting that if one is honest because "honesty pays," he is not acting morally but is acting for profit. *Animals* act for profit. Humans, however, have a sense of the unconditional in certain circumstances. To respond from the sense of unconditional obligation is what makes a person uniquely human.

One well-known illustration of this principle comes from the writings of Mencius, Confucius' best-known successor:

> All men have a mind which cannot bear to see the suffering of others. . . . If now men suddenly see a child about to fall into a well, they will without exception experience a feeling of alarm and distress. . . . From this case we may perceive that he who lacks the feeling of commiseration is not a man; that he who lacks the feeling of shame and dislike is not a man; that he who lacks a sense of right and wrong is not a man.[3]

A human being feels a sense of unconditional obligation to save a child in danger. What marks the person as human is the element of unconditionality about his motive. He is not motivated by profit,

---

[3]Mencius

reward, praise or honor. Rather, the sense of an absolute obligation to save the child calls from inside him. This is morality, Confucius maintained.

Man is acting at his best when he acts morally. There are times when a person is motivated by profit. But there are also times when the issue of profit should be set aside, when a person should consider doing something for its own sake. The gentleman—one who exhibits manhood at its best—is the one who responds properly to this inner sense of obligation.

Some distinctions are worth bearing in mind. Some acts might be worth doing, but they have no moral content to them at all (as when a Boy Scout works merely to earn a merit badge). And there are acts which are moral but which seem unprofitable, unrewarded, and even personally disastrous. And there are even occasions where a moral act will be rewarded. What is important in this final case is that the act be motivated by the sense of obligation. Only that inner sense of the unconditional makes an act moral.

> A great man is not bent on having his words believed nor on making his actions effective. He takes his stand on righteousness (*yi*), nothing else.[4]

THE SUPPORTING DOCTRINES

Confucianism fills out the implications of yi by laying down ways in which the sense of unconditional obligation is to be expressed. The Confucianists were aware that if the individual is left with only the message that he must act according to a sense of unconditionality, he is soon perplexed concerning just what exactly he should do. One might know immediately what to do when a child is seen about to fall into a well. But what does one do for one's parents when they are old and feeble? How does one express friendship and loyalty in complicated situations? How does one know what deeds properly express the sense of unconditional obligation?

Confucianists addressed these issues by turning to the ancient texts. The classical books spelled out a formal way of living which properly expresses human obligation, it was thought.

One strong theme found in the ancient books is the theme of filial piety (hsiao). Filial piety is a reverence and respect for parents and ancestors. This is the area where the sense of obligation is felt most acutely. After all, each person is unconditionally obligated to parents.

---

[4]Mencius

You or I would not exist were it not for a mother and a father. Each person is absolutely, unconditionally dependent upon parents. So parents deserve reverence, respect and obedience—with no assurance that such reverence, respect or obedience will be rewarded. Parents deserve it because of *who* they are, not because of what they do or how well they fulfill their role as parents.

Acts of reverence toward parents are to be done as moral obligation. "The duty of children to their parents is the fountain from which all virtues spring," said Confucius. And Chinese folklore abounds with stories to illustrate this principle. One story tells of the plight of a young couple during a time of famine. The young man's mother, as well as their young son, lived with the couple. The time finally came when a decision had to be made concerning which of them would starve. There simply was not enough for all to eat. The young man decided that his young son should starve. His reasoning was based on the insight that while he and his wife could always have another son, he could never have another mother! One's obligation to a parent is unconditional. Such reasoning was considered by Confucianists to be a model of moral reasoning.

Yet another principle mined from the classics is that of human-heartedness (*jen,* pronounced "wren"). This obligation for moral behavior is felt toward other people. Since a person knows what it is to be treated with decency, dignity and respect, each person has an inner guide for conduct with others. "Do not do to others what you do not want done to yourself," Confucius said. The rule is to use one's own sense of dignity and worth as a standard by which to treat others. What might be disrespectful, undignified, or short-sighted if done to oneself should never be done to another.

Yet another clue to proper behavior is the principle of the mean (*chung yung*). Proper behavior is never extreme. It always is marked by appropriateness, balance, deliberation. An English word which connotes the same idea is "temperance." Temperance avoids extremes of overindulgence or self-denial. It lives a careful, regulated, controlled and balanced life.

The Confucian reverence for ancient texts contributed to a style of life which put great importance upon the past. Through an understanding of the past, the Chinese sought a model for the perfection of society. Words, ideas, strategies, and styles were all to be culled from the ancient books and used as a model for reconstructing society. The teachers' task was to point students to the past. The students' task was to learn the past and then to put into practice what was learned. Learning the past meant learning the proper meaning of words.

What is a "father"? What is a "son"? What is a "ruler"? And what is a "subject"? Answers to these questions emerge from the ancient texts. The gentleman's responsibility is to discover the proper meanings of words and to put them into practice through behavior and through social institutions.

The significance of Confucian thought for China was that it provided a structure for social and political life which functioned for centuries. One might expect that specific rulers of China were as corrupt and self-seeking as rulers anywhere might be. But once Confucian teaching was officially adopted as government policy, the ideal was carried in theory as an inseparable part of Chinese civilization. Some scholars have argued that China flourished under legalist principles cloaked in a garb of Confucian piety. Nevertheless, rulers were advised that capacity to govern has no necessary connection with birth, wealth, or even power. Instead, it rests upon character. The people of a nation respond with loyalty and allegiance to someone they sense is moral and upright. Trust cannot be forced or bought. It must be elicited by moral example. So the only way for a ruler to successfully hold together a state is by moral example. Thus, government from the top down was to be motivated and managed by principles of morality.

Confucian theory is difficult to criticize. Many have criticized it, but have ignored the theory itself, looking instead to see how well it was applied in Chinese society. The application of Confucian theory falls far short of the ideals about which it speaks. Confucianism built a civilization impressive in many respects. But it never realized the ideal order that it preached.

The shortcomings of Confucian theory itself fall into two distinct areas for consideration, both of which leave Confucianism vulnerable to criticism from the outside. The first and most obvious area of criticism concerns its anti-democratic and aristocratic cultivation of a cultural elite. The second area of criticism has to do with the soundness of the moral reasoning which provides the foundation for Confucian thought and culture.

The elitist criticism was fundamental to the Marxist and Maoist rejection of Confucianism. But nearly everyone who has absorbed democratic principles of social order would find it compelling. Confucianism puts strong emphasis upon developing people into "ideal" gentlemen. But not all can become gentlemen. Those who "make it" live a privileged life of refined taste and cultural sensitivity. The gentleman is knowledgeable, sensitive, skillful in writing and in debate, and also magnanimous (he can stand above injury and abuse). Since he needs nothing, he is free to give of himself or to withhold himself according to his inner sense of appropriate behavior.

The gentleman's refinement and taste come at the expense of everyone else who cannot attain such position. In his sensitivities and learning, the gentleman is far removed from the cares and concerns of ordinary people. He stands as a model of "manhood-at-its-best." And ordinary folk do well, it is taught, to emulate him and strive toward attaining such personal qualities.

Most people influenced by democratic ideas about equality and the rights of the common man see something wrong with the Confucian elitism which raises a few people to a level where they are considered to be somehow "better" than others. For Marxist critics of China's Confucian past, the scholar-gentleman is the symbol of all that was repressive, oppressive, and exploitative about the old system which was overthrown.

The criticism of Confucianism based upon an examination of the moral foundations of the teaching is more complicated. The argument declares that the Confucian emphasis upon an inner sense of obligation as the fundamental ground of moral behavior is inappropriate. To identify morality with an inner sense of obligation is to limit morality to concerns about intuition, motives, and feelings. But morality has to do with actual deeds and acts in the world, it is argued.

What makes an act morally right or wrong, good or bad, lies in the nature of the act itself or in its consequences. The motive for doing the act is irrelevant to the moral value of the act. What is important is the act itself. One must ask, "Does this act measure up to some objective standard of good or bad, right or wrong?" or "Are the consequences of the act good or bad?" Many think these are the important questions to ask about morality since no one has access to another's motives or inner sensibilities. They claim Confucian teaching about morality removes morality from the area of public discussion and makes it a matter of private sensitivity.

The issue concerning the nature of morality is an important one, and Confucianism does raise it. What is the most important element in morality? Is it the motive for the act? Is it the act's correspondence to a universal standard of right and wrong? Or is it the consequence of the act which is the important consideration? What is it that makes an act a moral act?

A person's decision on these questions positions him within one of a number of traditions of moral reasoning. Confucianism raises the issue and advocates a position. And it built a civilization upon the conviction that people can be educated to an inner moral sensitivity which will (with the help of the ancient texts) produce a harmonious, orderly, and moral society.

Signs indicate that the modern world has little interest or time to devote to educate people in such sensitivities; too many other matters press for attention. Confucianism's fate in the modern world is tied up with the cultivation of the "gentlemanly" qualities. Can Confucianism thrive in an age of science, technology, and international economic competition?

RECOMMENDED READING

Creel, H. G. *Chinese Thought from Confucius to Mao-Tse Tung.* Mentor, 1953.
Danto, Arthur. *Mysticism and Morality.* Basil Books, 1972.
Frank, Wolfgang. *China and the West.* Harper, 1967.

Chapter 3

THE TAOIST ALTERNATIVE

Alongside the official state teaching of Confucianism lived the mystical teachings of Taoism (pronounced "Dowism"). The two religious movements contradicted one another in nearly every teaching. But they shared assumptions of a natural order and a Golden Age when mankind lived well. They disagreed on how to return to the natural order of the Golden Age and what style of living might characterize such an age.

Taoism had two origins which can be traced. Some philosophers of the time of Confucius insisted that there is a *Tao*, a "Way," for humans to live which is natural to human beings. Even as plants, insects, and animals unreflectively live simply and naturally, so human beings can fall back into a natural way of living that is spontaneous, simple, peaceful, and natural. Such a way avoids conflict, disagreements, jealousy, greed, and war. Creating governments, institutions, laws, and administrative procedures is a mistake. The way of the universe is natural, unreflective, spontaneous. Human philosophies and theories of order are artificial constructions superimposed upon nature. The imposition of what is unnatural and artificial is a mistake. And all the disorder experienced by mankind results from people imposing wrong ideas upon nature.

A second source for Taoism lay in the work of shamans and magicians who achieved both popularity and credibility among the masses of China with their promises of increased power and immortality. At the popular level of culture, these teachings were a crude amalgam of superstition, alchemy and primitive biology.

The two movements combined at some point to create a religion of mysticism that was influential in the everyday life of the masses who remained cut off from most of the "learning" of the Confucianists. Combining popular superstitions with a more philosophical contemplation of nature's way came about rather easily. The philosophers of nature were bound to pass from a simple observation of nature to experimentation with nature. Once such a step is taken by someone there is little distinction to be made between the high abstractions of a philosopher concerning the ways of nature and the work of an alchemist or shaman stoking his furnace to prepare the pill of immortality. This is simply a move from speculation about nature to some specific acts done to control nature. Chinese religious thought demonstrates that there is but a short distance between speculative science and magic: the only difference is the level of skepticism involved in the experiments. Both attempt to bring about changes to the advantage of men.

But there is a considerable distance between the attitudes expressed in the ancient Taoist writings and the later Taoist "discoveries" of potions, chemicals, and processes alleged to bring immortality. It should be noted that official Confucian teaching held only contempt for what Taoists both taught and did. One reason a modern science never developed in China was that official scholarship would have nothing to do with experimentation. Once a person made a move toward the actual manipulation of nature, he stepped out of the established literary culture: manual work done by a scholar meant that he was no longer a scholar. He was ostracized. Hardly any established scholar would jeopardize his hard-won position in that way.

Thus Taoism, both as philosophical speculation and as a manual tinkering with tools and chemicals, never made a significant impact upon the social system of China. To be sure, stories abound of Chinese gentlemen scholars working for years in the bureaucracy only to drop out and take on the role of the Taoist philosopher. But such an act was literally a "drop out." It meant ostracism from the society of the educated and refined. Discoveries today of an ancient and neglected science indicate that the early philosophers of nature were surprisingly sophisticated in their knowledge of the natural world.

PHILOSOPHICAL TAOISM

Taoist thought holds a striking appeal for many today because of its penetrating criticism of the artificiality of contemporary life. Taoist criticism was its strongest in the face of a rigid Confucian orthodoxy. Yet three issues shaping Taoism hold striking relevance to modern thought.

The first issue was the view held by many thinkers during the time of social upheaval immediately preceding the rise of Confucianism, that the most important thing in the world is the preservation of one's own life and the avoidance of injury. This ancient text reads as though it were written only yesterday:

> Our life is our own possession, and its benefit to us is very great. Regarding its dignity, even the honor of being Emperor cannot compare with it. Regarding its importance, even the wealth of possessing the world would not be exchanged for it. Regarding its safety, were we to lose it for one morning, we would never again bring it back. On these three points those who have understanding are careful.[1]

Two principles stand out in considering this strand of Taoist concern: (1) Each man is wise to live for himself first (rather than to devote himself to the service of family or society). (2) Life is to be valued more than possessions or ideas. There is nothing more important in the world than one's own life, for without it, there is nothing!

A second issue contributing to Taoist philosophy was the crisis of language that occurred some time around the fifth century B.C. Thinkers discovered that words tend to move in a world pretty much of their own, often unconnected to the world of material reality. The nature of Chinese language itself might have had something to do with this concern (a concern about language is also central to philosophy in the twentieth century).

Chinese as a system of writing is surprisingly different from Western languages: It has no alphabet, no spelling, no grammar, no parts of speech. There are no inflections, declensions, conjugations, cases, numbers, tenses, or moods. Every word may be a noun, a verb, an adjective, or an adverb. Context, tone, and accompanying gestures determine the precise meaning of a word.

Each Chinese word sound of one syllable can be pronounced with four to nine tones. When a word is spoken, its specific tone indicates the meaning of the word. But a Chinese word written on paper does not carry the tone. For example, the word *Yi* may mean sixty-nine different things. *Shi* may mean fifty-nine different things. *Ku* may mean twenty-nine different things.

Early Chinese thinkers concluded that a word changes when it is put on paper. It becomes ambiguous, even misleading. A gap exists between speaking and writing, hearing and reading.

Written Chinese is made up of pictograms (shorthand marks for an object, a thing, or an action). There are about six hundred fundamental signs. The fundamental signs are connected to make up more complicated signs which stand for combinations of words or concepts. For example, "dog" has one sign. But "wild dog" has a combination of signs. And "wild dog running in the street" has another combi-

---

[1] Lu-chih Chún-Chíu

nation of signs. Once a person knows the fundamental signs and how they are connected with basic indicators which change the signs, he knows how to read.

But knowing how to read the signs does not mean that one knows how the signs are to be pronounced and spoken as words strung together. Thus the characters written and the words spoken are very different.

One conclusion Chinese thinkers reached when considering these matters was that there is only a casual connection between words and reality. Words move in a world that is meaningful only in terms of itself. A word means something because it is put into a context with other words. Words get their meanings from their relation to other words. And whether words actually refer to anything in the external world is questionable, these Chinese thinkers concluded.

They went even further than that. They alleged that it is a mistake to think that words are tied to reality. Words are artificial and purely conventional indicators, they insisted. The peculiar nature of Chinese as a written language forced many to the conclusion that words do not refer to anything real except other words.

Speculation about language resulted in three proposed solutions to the problem of language. And each proposed solution became associated with a major school of Chinese thought. The Confucianists responded to speculation about language by insisting upon their doctrine of the Rectification of Names. These held that there had been an original correspondence between words and things, and words and reality. But language had decayed to the point of being disarranged and imprecise. Confucianists insisted that we need to go back to the past to discover the original meanings of words, and then to arrange life so that it corresponds to the correct meanings. Access to the original meanings comes through attention to the classical texts. There we can discover what "father" actually means, what "ruler" actually means, what "son" actually means. The Confucianists insisted that the solution to the decline of proper standards in society is the rectification of words so that they are made to correspond to reality. And that can be done if attention is given to the ancient books.

A second solution was proposed by the Legalist and Mohist thinkers. Both schools advocated a doctrine of Unification of Standards. In their view, the ruler ought to determine the meanings of words and force all people in the state to conform to such meanings. The ruler must do this in every sphere of social life. He must determine what is meant by a pound of wheat, an ounce of gold, an acre of land, a mile of road. The task of good government is to unify such standards.

But Unification of Standards must extend to human conduct and relations.

Both Legalist thinkers and Mohist thinkers claim that any crisis of language arises from incompetent rule. Government must extend itself to the legal control of language itself.

Taoist thinkers, however, concluded something quite different about the nature of language. They insisted that names and words are relative. Words describe or name something only in terms of something else (even if the "something else" is not specifically mentioned). No thing is itself either "long" or "short." What someone means by "long" or "short" is implied by the context of words in which "long" or "short" are used. The meaning of a word is implied by an immediate frame of reference in which a word is spoken or written. And the frame of reference is always relative to other frames of reference. What is a "long" flight to a sparrow is but a "short" flight to a migrating duck.

Words do not have absolute meaning, Taoists insisted. They are relative, incomplete, inaccurate, and often deceptive. The use of language is at best only a game. The game has its rules, as does every game. And if a person wants to play the game, he must play by the rules. But language is merely a game. As with many games, it might be a fun diversion for children, but there must come a time in life when a person chooses to move beyond games.

A third issue which contributed to Taoist thought is the view that there is no clear purpose to life. The social chaos of early China surely contributed to such a view. Yet it became a view which received some theoretical backing. The argument was that observation of events in the world show (by themselves) no ultimate purpose for their taking place.

One might answer the question of why something happens by looking at what caused it to happen. But one cannot find any purpose for it taking place, no final object. Events might be put to some use, they might be given some immediate purpose by clever men. One might use the occurrence of a famine to overthrow a king. But one cannot say that the *purpose* of famines is to overthrow kings. No overarching grand purpose for events is revealed by observing events themselves.

These thinkers insisted that any method of explaining events by appealing to some ultimate purpose rests upon some source other than observation. Appeal to purpose in explaining events, therefore, is unjustified, these thinkers said.

An ancient story illustrates this view. A twelve-year-old boy objected to his banquet host's speech in which the host had explained that heaven makes the grain to grow and animals to live so that men might flourish. There is a grand purpose in the world, he said. Nature exists to supply food for mankind. Things are ordered by heaven so that nature exists for man's good. Man, he insisted, is the end for which all other things are made.

The young boy objected, saying that it is only man's size, strength, and intelligence that gives him mastery over other forms of life. None of these things by themselves show that they exist to serve man's interests. Mosquitos and gnats suck man's blood; wolves devour human flesh. But would his host like to argue that heaven produced mankind as food for mosquitos, gnats, and wolves?

The purpose of things is relative to a particular point of view, a particular frame of reference, the boy argued. What seems to be a fine purpose for the existence of a cow (food for man) might not seem so fine a purpose from the cow's viewpoint. In short, these thinkers insisted, the world itself does not indicate that it was made for man or that man is the preeminent form of life in the world.

The modernity of these issues contributing to Taoism is striking. Concern for self-fulfillment and self-realization over against social responsibilities, a skepticism concerning the reliability of language to correspond to reality, and doubting that there is any final purpose to life is viewed by some modern thinkers as peculiar to our time. Since Chinese thinkers went through a similar crisis two thousand years ago, some turn for guidance and solace to the major Taoist text, the Tao Te Ching (The Way and Its Power).

THE WAY AND ITS POWER

The earliest complete Taoist text, called Tao Te Ching, is attributed to a man called Lao Tzu. Who he was, when he lived, and whether he actually wrote the book are all questions open to debate. The name Lao Tzu is simply a term of familiar respect, meaning "Old Master," or even "Old Boy."

Though not much is known of the man who is thought to have written the book, the book itself is available for easy perusal, since it is maybe the most translated book of Chinese lore. Yet the number of translations testify to the book's ambiguity. It is difficult to find any two translators agreeing on how to put the Chinese words into English.

The book emerges from a concern over the issues described above. The first lines of the book say:

The Way that can be told of is not the Absolute Way. The names
that can be named are not the Absolute Names.

In short, the book argues that something is fundamentally incorrect in assuming that language provides an accurate and reliable description of reality. Something is wrong in assuming that language
can declare rules for appropriate moral conduct in the world. It is
foolish, the book insists, to think that words can state the principles
of proper government in the world.

Skepticism about language, morals, and government emerges from
a view that the Way (the *Tao*) of the universe cannot be grasped by
the intellect. The universe proceeds, it moves, it does what it does.
But it cannot be grasped intellectually or expressed in words. It can
only be experienced. It cannot be described.

Yet the *Tao Te Ching* does provide some general hints as to the
Way of the universe. The book suggests that the Way is immanent;
it is the driving force within nature. It is transcendent; it is beyond
the capacity of the intellect. It is the norm; it is the way all things in
nature operate, including mankind.

Though one might wish to object to any attempt to put into words
what is claimed to be inexpressible, the book does go on to characterize how people should live individually and socially. People should
adjust life so that it conforms to the *Tao*, the book claims. Adjusting
to the *Tao* is to conform to a type of action in the world which can
be characterized as "nonaction" (a way of living suggesting that natural inclinations and spontaneity should determine how one acts in
the world). Adjusting government to the *Tao* of the universe would
be to rule by nongovernment (letting society exist without rules or
laws). And adjusting personal life to the *Tao* would be to live with a
simplicity unencumbered by technology (a return to nature). And all
of this is proposed as the proper solution to the dissolution of social
order occurring in ancient China.

To follow Lao Tzu's advice is to live according to the way of the
universe, a way which is nameless, yet perfectly natural. It is to be
in harmony with the force behind the world from its beginning, the
force which all things in nature follow.

Human life made to conform to the *Tao* is characterized in the
book as *Wu Wei* ("nonaction" or "inaction"). Essentially it means to
refrain from any activity which is contrary to nature, to avoid going
against the grain, to shun any attempt to force people or materials to
do things for which they are unsuited. *Wei* means "to force things,"
to make things do something against their intrinsic principles. *Wu
Wei* means to let things work according to their intrinsic principles.

The *Tao* is observed through the power and skill exhibited in nature. Nature does things without any apparent effort, without any tension. Water is an obvious case. It supports objects effortlessly. A swimmer knows that water will hold him up if he relaxes and does not struggle against it. Moreover, water always adapts to its surroundings, taking the shape of its container. It always fits into a glass or pitcher and takes the exact shape of the vessel. Yet in spite of its adaptability, its ability to accommodate itself to an immediate environment, it holds a great power. Water that flows around huge stones— conforming to them—wears them away to nothing in time.

Living in harmony with *Tao* means to realize one's intrinsic nature. It appears to be a life of accommodation, a life of weakness. But behind such a life is the force of the universe.

Human beings ought to conform to the selflessness and simplicity found in nature. They should have few desires. Food, clothing, shelter and community are needs easily met. But unnatural desires associated with fame, wealth, power over people are not easily met. Attempts to meet such desires bring trouble. Unnatural desires always lead to aggression, competition, strife. Natural desires lead to none of these. Even a child does not overindulge when eating, playing, or working. A child lives in a natural harmony with himself and his surrounding. A child must be taught to hurt himself by overindulgence, aggression, or labor.

The way of nature, then, should be the model for proper living. Laws, government, institutions are all unnatural creations which put unnatural demands upon people. The best way to live is to relax, to act spontaneously, unreflectively, unaggresively, naturally. And the best way to govern the state is not to govern at all.

CONFORMING TO THE WAY

The style of life advocated by Taoism follows from the insight that the universe is not some machine bolted together by some supernatural mechanic. It is an organic whole.

But the one organic whole which is the universe and its way carries polar forces called *Yin* and *Yang*. What we know of things in the world, we know because we see one thing being different from other things. What makes a specific thing stand out is the balance within the specific thing of the forces of *yin* and *yang*.

Yin is a characteristic in nature which expresses itself through femininity, passivity, coolness, darkness, wetness, earthiness. Water is almost a complete expression of *yin*.

Yang, on the other hand, exhibits characteristics of masculinity, activity, heat, light, dryness, and heavenliness (the bright blue sky, for example). Fire is almost a complete expression of *yang*.

Taoists insist that all things are comprised of the polar forces expressing *yin* and *yang*. The two are opposing tendencies, polar tendencies. Yet the two combine to make all things that exist in the world. The world itself is a balancing of the forces of *yin* and *yang*.

This means that all opposites in the world really depend upon one another. All things are actually interdependent, interrelated, relative to one another. Black is black because it is the opposite of white. Yet black depends upon white in order to be black. Male and female appear to be polar opposites. But each depends upon the other to make each what it is. This is the nature of all things in the universe, Taoists say.

Taoists draw a number of conclusions from this analysis of *yin* and *yang* being interdependent. First is the notion of the reversal of the *Tao*. This means that life and human events should never be seen in linear terms of progress toward some ultimate goal of history. Instead, history moves in a circle. History is a circle of events in which one expression is followed in time by its opposite. Summer always follows winter, and winter follows summer. They are opposite expressions of the forces of *yin* and *yang*. The way of the *Tao* is reversal. History is going nowhere but where things were before.

Second, Taoists insist, there is implied in the notion of the relationship of *yin* and *yang* the relativity of truth. There can be no absolute truth about the world because everything implies its polar opposite, its contrary. Every idea contains its own negation or opposite. And every idea is relative to a context and a time. To try to explain the grandeur of the heavens to a well-frog whose sense of the sky is a little blue circle above him would be useless. Men considered Mao Chíang and Li Chi the most beautiful of women. But when a fish saw them, it dived deep into the water, birds soared high, and a deer ran away. Which of these creatures has the right standard for judging beauty? Values are relative.

Finally, Taoists maintain, morals are relative. Again, it is insisted, the context of a moral judgment determines the nature of the judgment. But contexts always change. So moral judgments are relative. What is good in one context might be bad in another context.

The typical story used to illustrate moral relativity is the story of the old farmer whose horse ran away one day. His neighbor heard about his misfortune and said, "That's bad." But the old farmer replied, "Who knows what is good or bad?"

The next day the horse returned, bringing with it six wild horses it had met in its wandering. The neighbor returned to say, "That's good!" But the old farmer replied, "Who knows what is good or bad?"

The next day the farmer's son broke his leg while trying to ride one of the wild horses. The neighbor appeared again, "That's bad!" he said. But the old farmer replied, "Who knows what is good or bad?"

The next day the soldiers of the landlord prince came around inducting young men into the army. The farmer's son was left with his father because he had a broken leg. The neighbor said, "That's good!" But the old farmer replied, "Who knows what is good or bad?"

The story implies that what is seen as good at one time or in one context can be seen as bad in another time or context. Taoists draw the conclusion that one ought not to make moral judgments. However, it should be pointed out that this story is not talking about moral issues. It speaks of good fortune and bad fortune. If this is noted, then the wisdom of the rustic farmer is not so unique. Times change and with the change in times, perspectives change. But wise men, ranging from Stoic philosophers to Christian saints, have insisted upon moral absolutes when counseling an attitude of resignation toward the uncertainties of life. Any persuasive argument for moral relativity would have to be based upon firmer footing than the story of the old farmer whose horse ran away. Analysis of the soundness and validity of moral statements must precede any conclusions concerning moral relativity. Yet Taoists wish to do away even with the words "good" and "bad"—and the story suggests that it is best to abandon them as meaningless terms. The *Tao Te Ching* says:

> First there was *Tao*,
> Then there was *Yin* and *Yang*.
> And then there were words.
> Oh, that men would have left it
> alone!

Taoism has little to say about ethics to anyone trained in the logical analysis of terms and propositions. Taoists insist upon the inability of language to express any truth with accuracy or precision. It is in poetry, painting, and music that Taoism has made its greatest contribution to Chinese culture. Most of the great artists of China were men who became dissatisfied with life in the world of Confucian scholarship and government work. The teaching of Taoism provided a complete contrast to the achievement oriented life of Confucianism.

In place of self-assertiveness, Taoists idealized humility, saying that the "axe always falls first on the tallest tree." Against the Confucianist tendencies to encourage management, standardization, and organization, Taoists chose to tune themselves to nature, to abandon city life, and to join the flow of nature—to accept the acts of nature as inevitable.

Taoists encouraged conformity to nature and contemplation of it. Poets and writers, usually officials and scholars who had "dropped out," spent their time absorbing the ways of nature as a means to gain inspiration for their work. Artists abandoned the city and spent as long as fourteen years observing nature before taking one brush stroke! The poet Táo Chíen was a Confucian scholar who left a government position because, he said, he could no longer "crook the hinges of my back for five pecks of rice a day." He abandoned city life and headed for the countryside.

> I pluck chrysanthemums under the eastern hedge,
> Then I gaze long at the distant summer hills.
> The mountain air is fresh at the dawn of day;
> The flying birds two by two return.
> In these things there lies a deep meaning;
> Yet when we would express it, words suddenly fail. . . .
> What folly to spend one's life like a dropped leaf
> Snared under the dust of streets!
> For a long time I have lived in a cage;
> Now I have returned.
> For one must return
> To fulfill one's nature.

The typical Taoist artist flouted conventions of Confucian propriety. Generally the artists let their hair grow long, refused to cut their beards, washed little, and drank much. They were known to be "cool"—surely one of the squarest terms used today, since it is at least 1700 years old. Reading, writing, painting, versifying, carousing, these men studiously ignored organized society and tried their best to live in harmony with what they thought to be the *Tao* of the universe.

Taoism, then, stood as a second religious alternative for China. Some would argue that neither Confucianism nor Taoism are "religious" alternatives since neither talks of God, sin, or salvation. Yet the ideas and ideals expressed in these traditions claim ultimacy. The message of each demands a response. And each assumes that the proper response is assent, agreement, even conversion.

Both demand that people reorder life, and both promise final fulfillment for those who do so. Both options have been aggressively opposed by the Maoist-Marxist regime of contemporary China.

Confucianism is nearly extinct today, except for some communities in Taiwan and in various countries of Southeast Asia. Taoism, however, saw a short revival in the West, not as a result of missionary activity by Chinese, but because of counterculture youth who were dissatisfied with American and European social life. Concern for self-realization over against social responsibility, suspicion that language is an artificial instrument of control, and denial of any transcendent meaning to life marked the culture which emerged from the 1960s and 1970s. Since these values are as old as China, we have reason to examine them for their appropriateness to modern life.

RECOMMENDED READING

Needhan, Joseph B. and Wang Ling. *Science and Civilization in China.* 4 volumes. Cambridge University Press, 1954–1965.

Waley, Arthur. *Three Ways of Thought in Ancient China.* Allen & Unwin, 1939.

Wing-Tsit, Chan. *Sourcebook in Chinese Philosophy.* Princeton University Press, 1963.

Chapter 4

THE FATE OF MODERN CHINA

Confucian teaching is a comprehensive religious, cultural, and political system. It served as a foundation for an amazing civilization. Marco Polo, an adventurer from Italy in the thirteenth century, made the first sustained contact with China for the West. He wrote a book describing the China he saw. But most people disbelieved what they read in his book.

Polo told of a social and political order so far advanced from Europe it seemed impossible. He maintained that no country East or West could compare with China's state organization, monetary, postal, educational, or transportation systems. These amazing systems welded together a disparate population into one great civilization.

In time Western nations surpassed China in industrial, economic, and military capability. The modern history of Chinese religions is bound up with the traumatic discovery by Chinese thinkers that they had been bested by people long thought to be uncivilized.

To gain a sense of the crisis of modernization for China, it is helpful to keep in mind what it meant to be a part of the Chinese civilization. The Chinese instilled through their educational system a view of their central significance in the world order that made it extremely difficult for any educated person to consider foreigners to be anything but barbarians.

The teaching handed on to students was *authoritarian*, expecting unquestioning obedience, and *ethnocentric*, claiming that China was the epitome of culture. This authoritarianism and ethnocentrism prevented Chinese leaders from adjusting easily to the impending modernization carried by increasing contacts and dependencies on Western nations.

The authoritarianism of traditional China was based in the family system. The Confucian doctrines concerning filial piety lay at the heart of Chinese morality. In practice, filial piety meant that a son owes obedience and respect to his parents, particularly his father. A son was to honor his father simply because he was a father, not for any other reason.

Filial piety provided the moral base for order within the empire. All relations between family members and between government officials were regulated by the principle that a subservient person owes obedience to someone of greater age or official position. The political system made such obligations clear. The Emperor was the Son of Heaven who ruled by the Mandate of Heaven. He possessed superior moral qualities—that is why he ruled. Beneath the Emperor were the scholars who served as government officials. They achieved their positions through the examination system linking the schools of China to the government hierarchy. A person achieved position by showing himself knowledgeable in the areas considered most important. These areas were the classical texts.

Ranged under the scholars were the landed nobles, merchants, skilled artisans, and the peasants who tilled the soil. The authoritarian ordering of society, though it was no caste system, made much of rank and its prerequisites. It was to be expected that such a social ordering based upon the authority of rank would clash with the democratic ideals of equality and natural human rights espoused by many of the Westerners who were China's agents of change.

The authoritarian social system was buttressed by an intellectual authoritarianism. The educational system shaped by Confucianism held that truth was the possession of antiquity. Any debate or disagreement concerning what was true or right had always been settled by appealing to the ancient texts. The assumption built into the system was that a perfect order for life had been realized in the Golden Age. That period was a model for the present.

Commitment to the authority of the past lay as the foundation of social advance for anyone aspiring to rise within the system. The academic examination system stood as the gateway to advancement. The system selected a scholar class to serve as functionaries of the government. These achievers held posts ranging from teaching in village schools to advising the emperor.

The content of the system's education was preoccupied with the past. It had little or nothing to do with administration, law, or management. Instructors emphasized knowledge of the classical writings. Study for the examination system required constant drilling in Confucian moral principles and in writing formal essays which applied those principles.

Thus China's educational system institutionalized an authoritarian view of knowledge. Truth was a possession of antiquity. To succeed in China was to pass the examinations. Passing the examinations required a detailed knowledge of the past. Independent thought or study, even a suggestion that some other sort of knowledge might be important, assured failure. A student did not rock the boat with new ideas or methods because the system was set up to throw him over- board if he did. The educational system demanded conformity to an unchanging ideal.

The authoritarian system of traditional China was accompanied by a strong ethnocentrism. The assumption that one's own culture and tradition are superior to all others is a characteristic of every society, no doubt. But in China ethnocentrism had been spelled out carefully. Just as the Pole Star remains fixed in the center of the heavens, so the central ruler on earth, the Emperor of China, is the immovable pole around which all mankind gathers. Moreover, the Emperor rules by the Mandate of Heaven. He stands as a link between heaven and earth, heaven and mankind. The dwelling place of the emperor is the center of the inhabited world, the source of order, culture and civilization. China, it was maintained, is the civilizing center of the world.

The Emperor rules because of his superior moral qualities and cultural sensitivity. Foreign states gather around the center. As dis- tance from the center increases, the standard of culture decreases. Imperial relations with foreigners must be conducted in ways that reflect this order. So certain principles of foreign relations came to be the norm upon which to base all conduct with foreigners.

A first principle is that the world order is *hierarchical,* based on rank, not *egalitarian,* based on equality. There is no such thing as legal equality or independent sovereignty of states or countries. World order requires a hierarchy, and China is naturally at the top of that hierarchy.

Second, China's position in the world order is because of her moral and cultural superiority. Order in the world is as much an ethical phenomenon as a political phenomenon. Harmony among countries was actually seen as a product of China's virtue. Because China realized moral virtue, there was order in the world, it was thought.

Third, the world hierarchy is universal. There is no other hier- archy, no other source of power on the international scene. Any con- cept of a "balance" of power is inconceivable. All foreign states are subservient to China, the teaching maintained.

Fourth, national power is a reflection of national virtue. Power follows from goodness. There is no conflict between "right" and "might." To the traditional Chinese thinker, "might" does not make "right." Rather, "right" makes "might." Those who are right will be strong. Any use of "might" is justified by its very existence; without "right" there would be no "might."

China's confrontation with Western nations in the eighteenth and nineteenth centuries constituted a shocking discovery that her authoritarian and ethnocentric attitudes were inappropriate assumptions against the reality of the modern world. China's crisis began when Western maritime powers moved into the waters off the coast of China and attempted to establish trade relations. The Portuguese made the earliest attempts in the late sixteenth century. But the Chinese authorities dismissed them to the small island of Macao, granting them legal immunity because they were convinced that Portuguese could not live under civilized law. The Dutch later enrolled themselves into the traditional tribute system, buying the right to trade with China.

But the British traders, with backing from their government, refused to compromise with Chinese views. London demanded free and uncontrolled access to Chinese ports and the establishment of a permanent representative in the capital to defend British trading interests. Great Britain finally went to war against China in the mid-nineteenth century to force open ports to British traders.

This occasion for a British display of superior might was the infamous Opium War of 1840–42. British gunboats sailed into Chinese harbors and forced China to accept shipments of opium in exchange for her exports. British forces overwhelmed the Chinese and extracted a series of treaties which began with British access to ports and ended with all European powers gaining access to China.

Military might forced China to her knees. Only then did China begin to reassess her claims to cultural superiority. Chinese thinkers who had ignored Western culture were forced by military might to recognize Western civilization.

Chinese scholars were not all convinced that high marks in military technology constituted high marks in matters of culture. What they did in the face of political and cultural disaster created intense controversy among the scholars.

Three groups emerged among the scholar-officials debating the rescue of China. One group advocated total revolution (a complete abandonment of the traditional way of life—including Confucianism). A second group insisted that a return to the "authentic" past was the only way to save China. China was not theirs to modernize and change; it had been passed on to them by their ancestors as a prized possession. A third group proposed a compromise between the old way of life and the new ideas thought to be necessary for survival in the modern world.

THE MODERNIST DILEMMA

By the 1890s China was no longer a land of complacent Confucian scholars cherishing a comfortable sense of moral superiority. Since European powers were chopping China into various spheres of domination, the overriding concern of the scholar-officials was survival as an independent nation in the new international situation. China's predicament suggested that something was fundamentally wrong with the basic ideas of their traditional way of life. The tendency was to discard traditional ways because they seemed unsuitable to the new situation.

How to create a strong China was a problem. Because China was overrun by foreigners intent upon taking all they could get from her, a nationalist movement asserting independence and sovereignty seemed to be the only solution. Building a sense of national pride and identity was difficult while at the same time admitting that China's old way of life was what had brought ruin. Nationalism requires a strong sense of a cherished past as a motive for unity and courageous action. But the Chinese were reminded daily that their past was no match against the foreigners. How could the Chinese cherish a past which had brought such embarrassment?

At the turn of the century a new generation of intellectuals insisted that a whole new social order must be constructed based upon new ideas imported from the West. These young revolutionaries insisted that the Chinese tradition was irrelevant to the modern world. A break with the past required two things: (1) Traditional Chinese beliefs and ideas must be abandoned. (2) Ideas from Western sources must be employed to build a new nation.

Widespread civil unrest finally toppled the empire in 1911. But the new government, a republic headed by (of all people) a former advisor to the late Empress Dowager Tz'u-Hsi (Ci Xi, Pinyin) rested upon a shaky foundation. In but a short while the president, Yuan Shih-K'ai (Yuan Shikai, Pinyin), made a move to install himself as a new emperor. Army generals turned against Yuan, and China fell into regional struggles for power among various warlords, each convinced that he was the one to return China to her past greatness.

A strong revolutionary movement did not emerge until the country was reducing itself to a shambles. The New Culture Movement took shape between 1915 and 1919. Ch'en Tu-hsiu (Chen Duxiu,

Pinyin) returned from exile in Japan to publish a magazine titled *New Youth*. He stressed that a complete cultural and moral transformation of society was a prerequisite for meaningful social reform and political action. All values, customs, and traditions of the past must be replaced by a wholly new culture based upon Western democratic and scientific principles. Ch'en insisted that the bearers of such a new culture must be the youth of the land. But they must build the new order upon a foundation of ideas, not simply upon revolutionary fervor. Social, economic, and political changes must be preceded by changes in ideas. A conversion from the old Confucianism to a scientific and democratic way of thinking must go before any other changes. Otherwise, he insisted, there would be revolution only for the sake of revolution.

The New Culture Movement took a strong interest in Marxism. The apparent success of Russian revolutionaries inspired by the Marxist theory seemed encouraging because the Russians had overthrown an old imperial order. Moreover, it was thought that Marxism was the most recent intellectual product of the modern West. China, if she could create a real socialist state, could go immediately to the head of the line and once again think of herself as the most civilized of nations. In addition, becoming a Marxist was one way for a Chinese intellectual to reject both the old way of life in China and the ways of the foreign intruders as well. And finally, to embrace Marxist doctrine was also to embrace a concrete program for political action promising to transform Chinese society.

It did not occur to the young intellectuals that the internationalist goals of Marxism clashed with and contradicted their own nationalist concerns. Nor did they comprehend that their concern for a united country did not fit well with Marxist demands for class struggle and revolution within society. Class struggle surely does not unite a society. And the issue of whether the peasant masses in the village and farms of the countryside might see any significance to the Marxist talk of class struggle between industry owners and workers did not concern the revolutionaries. Marxism, for the young Chinese revolutionaries, provided a suitable theory to explain why China was ground down by foreign powers at the same time as it promised the means to rise again to a position of strength in the world.

Alternatives to Marxism gained some ground when the American philosopher John Dewey and the British philosopher Bertrand Russell visited China's Peking (Beijing) University between the years 1917 and 1921 to lecture on the scientific bases for changing society. Dewey's Pragmatic-Scientific method of slow, experimental change appealed to some scholars who eventually sided with the republicanism of Sun Yat Sen and Chiang Kai-shek. Russell, however, lectured principally upon scientific theory. He met an audience with little grasp of what scientific theory might contribute to social change in China. The pressing need, it seemed, was some concrete proposal for action.

Marxism appealed to many younger, unhappy intellectuals of China who wanted immediate change. Of course it did not hurt the cause that Ch'en Tu-hsiu, China's chief spokesman for Marxism, was a dean at Peking University.

Yet China today is largely the result of a young peasant lad named Mao Tse-tung (Mao Zedong). He moved from the Hunan region of the south to the Peking area at just about the time controversies over social change raged on campus. Mao found a job in the university library and joined the Chinese Communist Party (CCP). His revolutionary commitment led him eventually to leadership of the CCP. And, in time, he took leadership of the world's largest nation.

THE HUMANISTIC APPEAL OF MARXISM

Mao's significance is difficult to overestimate. In fact, he may have achieved more in his lifetime than any man in modern history. At age 28 in a land of 400 million people, he joined, aided, and established a revolutionary movement designed to reorganize and reshape an entire culture and nation. Alexander, Caesar, Charlemagne, Napoleon, Bismark, Lenin—none could touch him in the scope of his accomplishment.

Yet Mao was merely an interpreter of Karl Marx. Seventy years before Mao, Marx and Engels published their *Manifesto of the Communist Party*. In it they laid out a description of what they saw taking place in the industrial cities of Europe. They coupled their observations with a theory of history that promised an eventual utopia. Moreover, they claimed their theory was scientific. They both described things actually taking place and predicted events which must follow as inevitable consequences. Thus the Marxist theory was presented as a scientific analysis and explanation of history.

Marxist theory contains two distinct elements and implies a third. First it lays down a theory called Historical Materialism (or sometimes, Dialectical Materialism). Second, it advances a description of economic relations within capitalist societies. And third, it implies a moral critique of human relations determined by capitalism.

Marx and Engels held that all human history must be understood as a history of competing material forces and interests. A movement begins. It meets an opposing force of interests which contradicts its claims. The two collide and a synthesis emerges from the collision of interests and claims. The synthesis becomes a new movement and soon meets opposition. The process of history is this dialectic: material interests meet opposing material interests (a thesis confronting an antithesis) which force a conflict among people and a synthesis emerges. But the synthesis becomes a new movement and the process repeats itself over and over.

Marx insisted that the dialectic is not between competing nations, states, or governments. Nor is the conflict that moves historical progression religious or philosophical. Instead, the actual process of history is a dialectic emerging from class conflict. Each person in the world belongs to a class group determined by the economic system that dominates a society. The economic system orders the means by which goods and services necessary for the society are produced and distributed. Thus, the most important element within the history of the world is the economic foundations upon which any particular society is based. The economy determines life because it is in economic relations that conflict always emerges.

For Marx, any man's class or position in a society is independent of his will or efforts. The economic system determines what a person's place is, what his future will be, even what his hopes might be. Each person is thrown into a class by the prevailing economic system of the production and distribution of goods. The economy controls life.

People living in a capitalist society fall into one of three social classes: (1) capitalist owners of industries; (2) workers; and (3) small business and service enterprises.

The dialectic at work in a capitalist society is a conflict which is the natural tension existing between the three groups. Capitalists live in constant tension with workers. Such tension is natural, since owners want to pay workers as little as possible and workers want to earn as much as possible. Between the capitalists and the workers stands a middle class of small businessmen. The middle class is caught between the economic interests on both sides of the conflict. In order to survive, the middle class must align itself with one side or the other.

Tensions necessarily increase in a highly industrialized society. Factories and machines bring greater increases in production. Capitalists increase their wealth because machines increase production at the same time as they replace workers. New machinery means that workers, on the whole, get poorer as they are replaced by machines. The capitalists, however, get richer because they have to pay fewer and fewer workers.

The economic theory used by Marx and Engels is the Labor The- ory of Value. In short, what gives a product its value in the market place is the amount of labor that goes into its production. The ordi- nary person wanting and needing to make enough money to live must sell his labor (literally himself and his time) to the capitalist owners of industry. The worker produces the goods which are then sold by the capitalist. For the capitalist to make a profit, he must pay the worker less than the price he asks for the product. The capitalist keeps the surplus value as a profit to do with what he will (surplus value is the money above what it costs the capitalist to hire workers and buy materials).

A simplistic illustration of the economic procedure at work is the story of the man who buys a tree which has fallen to the ground during a storm. He pays $1 for the tree. Then he finds a man who will cut the tree into firewood and stack it for $1. Finally, the capitalist sells the stack of firewood for $10. He makes a profit of $8 as surplus value. What gave the fallen tree its surplus value was the work of the man who cut it and stacked it. But the surplus value goes to the capitalist, the man who did nothing but put up some money to buy the fallen tree.

Two moral deficiencies of capitalist enterprise are implied in such a simplistic illustration. First, the worker is cheated: He makes the wood worth something, but he gets little in return for his contribu- tion. And second, when competition for cutting wood appears (sooner or later someone desperate enough to cut wood for less than $1 will appear), the worker's wages are driven down at the same time as the capitalist's profits increase.

Marxists insist that as competition occurs, tensions between the classes increase. Competition occurs also for the capitalist class. Some- one might appear who will sell a stack of cut wood for less than $10. So for the capitalist to survive, he must cut his costs by paying his worker less. Because of competition among capitalists, eventually only the richest among them survive. The rest are forced into bankruptcy and end up as workers themselves. And workers continue to be paid less and less as competition for jobs increases among them. It is in- evitable that workers will finally unite to overthrow the capitalist. The workers will install a new economic system. Marxists maintain that the new system will be socialism where the workers will own the means of production.

The moral theme within Marxism is evident. Capitalism as a sys- tem creates relations among people which are inhumane and immoral. It reduces relations among people to a competitive drive for profits.

And eventually that competition is a fight simply to survive. Human relations amount to nothing more than strategies for survival. The impersonal capitalistic economic system is to blame for such inhumane relations among people.

Capitalism does not make it possible for people to live more easily with greater security and prosperity, the theory implies. Exactly the opposite takes place. Capitalists compete across national borders to find cheaper labor and larger markets. Workers compete with one another to find jobs. Those who are lucky enough to find jobs must do work which is often dehumanizing. Workers in modern factories must compete with machines that work faster, longer, and cheaper than human beings. Thus relations with other people are destroyed as the economic system drives workers to compete against one another and against machines. Human beings become depersonalized and alienated from one another.

Though Marx and Engels put little emphasis upon the matter of alienation, the issue of alienation has been introduced as central to most contemporary interpretations of Marxist theory. The works of Eric Fromm, Jean Paul Sartre, and Maurice Merleau-Ponty make much of the idea that capitalist societies alienate man from his true self. People suffer the psychological trauma of alienation from their true selves because work in a capitalist society is labor with which they cannot identify. It is difficult for a person to take pride or satisfaction from his job screwing the same ½ inch screws into engine blocks day after day. Yet the industrial society requires just this sort of thing from countless workers. In the modern factory system what a person does to earn his daily bread has little or nothing to do with what he is as a real person, as a unique human being.

Such talk of alienation by the existentialist interpreters of Marx actually carries with it a contradiction of Marxist theory. Talk of alienation of a person from a "true" self, or soul, assumes that there is a real self which exists apart from the body doing work in the factory or work place.

But Marx and Engels, philosophical materialists, denied that there is anything more to a human being than a material body. All history, they maintained, must be understood only in terms of material bodies ordering economic interest. Human beings are economic beings dependent upon goods and services for survival. Microbes, insects, animals, and humans are no different in this respect: they are organisms dependent upon adequate food and shelter. It is foolish to think that humans possess a soul, they maintained.

The existentialist theme of alienation contradicts the Marxist teachings by asserting that there is a "self," or "soul," existing apart from the activities the body must do for survival. The existentialist theme does strengthen the ethical appeal of Marxism. Existentialists make much of the sense of "lostness" experienced by many who work in industrial settings. People can be characterized as "strangers" from themselves because they are forced to work at jobs which hold no personal meaning.

Yet it is important to remember that anyone holding to Dialectical Materialism cannot for logical reasons talk about a "true" self which is thought to exist apart from the material necessities of life. Dialectical Materialism asserts that there is no soul or independent self. It is therefore logically impossible to hold to both Dialectical Materialism and the existentialist ethical criticism. The two are incompatible.

Marx and Engels, however, did write about religion as a factor within the dialectic produced by a capitalist economy. Religion, they held, is a system of ideas and moral teachings constructed to defend the interests of the capitalist class. "All modern religions are instruments of bourgeois reaction that serve to defend exploitation and drug the working class," they maintained. Religion is one of many tools used to keep workers in their place. It promises "pie in the sky bye and bye" for those who remain submissive and uncomplaining.

Religion is but a by-product of the economic situation, Marx and Engels maintained. It teaches a morality of humility, obedience to one's betters (those who are powerful and rich), and passive acceptance of life as "God's will." It emphasizes piety instead of critical knowledge; it holds that the virtues of humility and peaceableness are more important than knowledge. It emphasizes individual and personal moral issues instead of impersonal social and economic issues that crush workers. It conceals the individual worker's sense of alienation from others by encouraging a relationship with God rather than relations with other people. Marx and Engels maintained that religion is an opiate that makes working people feel somewhat better about their unhappy situation.

Chinese intellectuals saw Marxist theory as both an accurate description of what had happened to their great civilization and a solution to their new sense of inferiority among the nations of the world. The theory put blame upon no person or nation. China's situation was produced out of the forces of the dialectic. Only the economic system can be blamed. All other issues of repression, servitude, weakness, dependency follow from the dialectic in which the old system is facing new forces. So the system must be destroyed. And any who wish to protect or preserve the system must be destroyed along with it.

The dialectic works toward a resolution of the conflict of interests between capitalists and workers, Marxists insisted. It is inevitable that a revolution occur in China. It must happen. And there are good moral reasons to help it along, regardless of how many must be destroyed in the process. Many Chinese intellectuals decided to line up on the side of Marx and Engels who said that revolution was the inevitable outcome of conflict between capitalists and workers of the world.

MAO'S INTERPRETATION OF MARXISM

Chinese thinkers were not troubled that the Marxist theory was a product of nineteenth century European industrial conditions. The theory promised a chance for China to once again step to the head of the line where social thought is concerned. Nor did it trouble the revolutionaries that Chinese religious life was influenced by Buddhist monasticism (which could not easily be considered a tool of capitalists) and Taoist withdrawal from the world (a conscious *rejection* of capitalist values of hard work and material wealth). The young revolutionaries eagerly wanted change—an overthrow of the Confucianist system that had dominated China for centuries. They cared little for overall consistency in their application of Marxist theory to Chinese social life.

Ch'en Tu-hsiu, dean at Peking University, founded the Chinese Communist Party in 1922. Party officials welcomed advisors from Russia to assist in showing how Marxist theory applied to Chinese life. Ch'en Tu-hsiu soon issued an official manifesto calling for workers and peasants to collaborate with the bourgeois Republican Party (called Kuomintang) led by Sun Yat Sen and Chiang K'ai-shek. Their united effort would rid the country of foreign oppressors and establish a solid national base. Then, after a reorganization of the state government, the Manifesto maintained, the real revolution between workers and capitalists would take place.

The strategy of Ch'en proved to be a disaster. Chiang K'ai-shek in 1927 took advantage of Communist Party member affiliation with his Kuomintang Party. He isolated Communist Party members, and ordered them slaughtered. The Communist Party nearly disappeared in major cities of the south. Only then did Mao's rise to prominence begin.

Mao's initial work took place in the southern countryside where he worked to unite peasants against the landlord class. Mao and the peasants experienced remarkable success in a series of revolts. They confiscated land from the wealthy landlords and redistributed it to peasants, even though orthodox Marxist theory opposed private ownership of property.

The successful revolts of peasants surprised many people. And Mao wrote in his famous tract, "Report on an Investigation of the Hunan Peasant Movement," that Marxist theory must be modified to meet the peculiar conditions of China. Industrial workers were not the key to the revolution in China, he maintained. Peasants who worked the land were the key. And they were about to take on the role of a revolutionary army.

> In a very short time, in China's central, southern, and northern provinces several hundered million peasants will rise like a mighty storm, like a hurricane; a force so swift and violent that no power, however great, will be able to hold it back. They will smash all the shackles that bind them and rush forward along the road to liberation. They will sweep all the imperialists, warlords, corrupt officials, local tyrants, and evil gentry into their graves.

Orthodox Marxists considered Mao's message heretical. Marxist theory had little to say about peasant farmers. Revolution was to occur among urban industrial workers. Mao's concern for peasants earned him official censure from party headquarters. Yet Mao gained the backing of thousands of liberated peasants.

Mao continued revising Marx in his essay "On Contradictions." He wrote this while holed up in the mountains of Yenan in 1937, after fleeing the armies of both Chiang K'ai-shek and the invading Japanese. Mao maintained that every society has its material-economic contradictions, its contrary forces. A dialectic is at work everywhere. But not every society has the same revolutionary contradictions. The job of the Marxist theorist is to scrutinize a society to discover the dominant contrary forces and then to discover at what point contradictions should be exploited to affect radical change. Revolutionary solutions differ according to situations of conflict.

Mao insisted that China had a number of conflicts within its society. The contradictory interests between the Chinese people and the outside foreigners exploiting China was an evident contradiction. Yet there were also the contradictions between the old feudal landlord class and the peasant masses. A contradiction between the new industrial capitalists and the workers existed as well. And finally, there was even a contradiction between the economic interests of the industrial workers of the cities and the peasants of the countryside.

Each conflict requires a different strategy for resolution, claimed Mao. Each demands its own response. If the Communist Party puts its attention upon the wrong conflict with an inappropriate strategy, the dialectic shaping history will not support the efforts of the Party. Thus, the major conflict of Chinese society must be discovered and exploited with an appropriate strategy. Only after the major conflict is resolved should attention be turned to other conflicts.

China's situation is different from the situations of Russia, Europe, or America, Mao asserted. China needs to revolt first against the foreign imperialist powers. He saw the Japanese military invasion of 1931 as the most vicious and visible force of domination by outsiders. Thus a nationalist war is of major concern. But then, Mao maintained, the masses of peasants must revolt against the feudal landlords to receive justice. Only after the landlords have been eliminated would the situation be ripe for a revolt of urban workers against industrialists. The last conflict would result in a socialist revolution that would place workers and peasants in a position of economic control. A natural conflict would continue to exist between peasants and workers, but such a conflict requires no violence. Economic interests of peasants and workers are similar. A dialectic of debate and discussion will sort out differences between peasants and workers, Mao said.

Mao wrote much more than tracts calling for a correct analysis of social conflict. He also wrote essays on the theory of knowledge (an attempt to avoid sterile speculation by insisting that all knowledge be grounded in practice), on aesthetics, on economics, and on government. He stressed the need for political education of the masses so that they might know how to probe the conditions of a society to discover where contradictions lie. Throughout his work the quest for a perfect society remains. It is the same quest which dominated traditional Chinese literature.

Mao's brand of Marxism is largely an ideology which fills the vacuum left by the dissolution of the old Confucian system of moral order. It reverses the older doctrines without losing the goal, that of establishing a proper social order. Dialectical Materialism explains what has happened to China and what is occurring in the world at large: material economic forces are confronting one another. The economic theory explains what needs to be done to correct the situation of injustice, oppression, exploitation, and national poverty that China inherited from the past. The ethical teaching implicit to the Marxist theory maintains that goodness is something which can be realized in society by reordering it according to principles of economic justice and equality.

Many see a moral idealism in much of Mao's writing. And strangely, the moral ideals parallel much of what Confucian morality had emphasized at the same time as the new ideals counter the old. Whereas Confucianists called for the gentleman's dedication to the improvement of society by drawing society toward the lofty ideals by which he lived, Mao calls for Party workers to give themselves unreservedly to the betterment of specific social conditions. The call to pursue what is right over against what is of mere personal profit occurs over and over, though "right" is redefined by Mao. The old Mandate of Heaven idea is replaced by the iron law of Dialectical Materialism. The emperor with his bureaucracy of scholar-gentlemen is replaced by the members of the Chinese Communist Party, representatives of the people, who are agents of harmony as they exploit the law of Dialectical Materialism. And the old goal of Confucian religion—that of collective harmony within the state—Mao promised as the result of new social measures to enforce equality and justice. The specific content of the system has been changed by Mao; but the function of the system has not. The ideal Mao aimed to achieve is harmony.

Maoism is the new religion of China. Its popularity comes from what it manages to restate in modern terms. It demands faith in an ideology that promises a social salvation. It carries an ethic not of private inner sensitivity to obligation but a public morality advocating equality and justice in society. Like most religions, Maoism offers an explanation for everything important that occurs in history. It provides the common man a sacred book, the "Little Red Book" of Mao's sayings. And it proclaims a hope for social salvation throughout the world as an inevitable result of the dialectic.

But neither Maoism nor Marxism is a science, though they both claim to be. Neither system tolerates fundamental questions, contrary evidence, or dissent concerning doctrines. Neither opens the door to new ideas, methods, or procedures in social and political life. And neither is able to even hint at what sort of empirical data might falsify its claims.

Maoism and Marxism are dogmas as rigid and inflexible as any ever produced in the history of religions. A science proceeds not by dogmas but by an open method whereby explanations or hypotheses are constantly subjected to tests aimed at falsifying them. Science must rest its conclusions upon the tentative grounds that data has not yet been found to nullify its conclusion. Conclusions are held only so long as they have not yet been falsified by new data or new tests.

Yet Maoists and Marxists refuse to subject their doctrines to tests

which might falsify them. Instead, they hold dogmatically to the doctrines of their past authorities: Marx, Engels, Lenin, and Mao. People
are asked or forced to believe that Marx, Engels, Lenin, and Mao
were correct in their assertions.

RECOMMENDED READING

Fitzgerald, C.P. *The Birth of Communist China*. Pelican, 1964.

Levinson, Joseph P. *Confucian China and Its Modern Fate*. 3 volumes.
University of California Press, 1958.

Lifton, Robert Jay. *Revolutionary Immortality. Mao Tse Tung and the
Chinese Cultural Revolution*. Vintage, 1968.

Spence, Jonathan D. *The Gate of Heavenly Peace. The Chinese and
Their Revolution, 1895–1980*. Penguin, 1981.

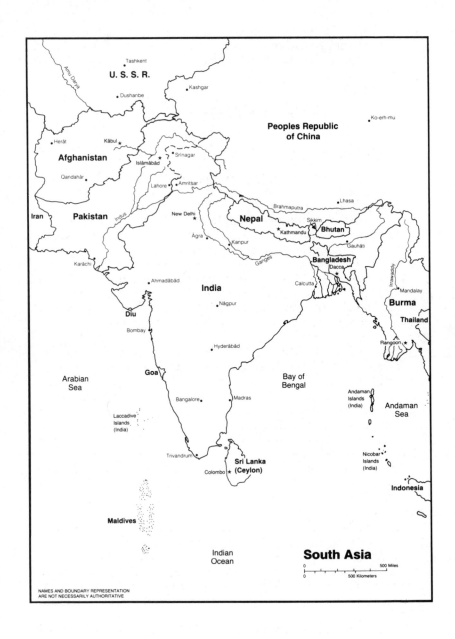

Chapter 5

THE STRUCTURE OF HINDU RELIGION

The modern world owes the discovery of Hindu religion to a British commercial venture. The British East India Company, a trading company of adventurous capitalists chartered by the British crown, established itself as a chief conduit of Asian exotica to Western Europe in the mid-eighteenth century. British success in trade did not come without vicious competition that left both Indians and Europeans altered. But Britain soon made herself an empire by opening markets both for her own products in Asia and for Asian commodities in Europe.

British Parliament in 1772 ordered a reform of company operations and sent Warren Hastings as viceroy to Calcutta. Hastings' reforms consisted of an effort to orientalize the company. He encouraged the men in the field to learn Indian languages and assume responsibility to Indian customs. Reform measures supported study of Indian languages and culture by offering financial rewards and advancement to those who could translate company procedures into Indian languages and law.

Mastery of Indian languages introduced some Englishmen to the literature of traditional India. While company interests encouraged first the study of local languages, the Hindu sacred language of Sanskrit also came to the attention of company men. With the discovery of Sanskrit literature, a new appreciation of Hindu culture and religion traveled to Europe. Discovery of Sanskrit led many East India Company men to the conclusion that somewhere, in a remote and uncharted period of history, lay a Golden Age of Indian culture. Some enthused that Sanskrit was a language "more perfect than Greek, more copious than Latin, and more exquisitely refined than either. . . ."

Such early impressions and conclusions about ancient India led

many European scholars into serious study of India's past. They became convinced that India did possess a Golden Age of civilization
which lay buried beneath centuries of neglect, priestly obscurancy,
and alien repression. The implied task of any student of language and
history was the unearthing of this ancient culture. Many Englishmen
attempted just that.

The circumstances of discovery of India are important to keep in
mind when studying Hindu religion. Knowledge of that ancient culture has been largely the result of European research. In other words,
most of what is known of the Hindu religious tradition has been
ferreted out by Englishmen. Thus India has been pulled through the
knothole of British intellectual history. When Englishmen studied
Sanskrit, they immediately compared it to Greek and Latin, the languages they associated with classical learning. When they formulated
interpretations of Indian ideas, they turned directly to the philosophers of ancient Greece and Rome for categories of explanation. Even
when Indian intellectuals later took up the project of rediscovering
India (or when other European scholars studied India), they too turned
to the categories of Western learning for help in unravelling and
explaining the complexities of ancient Hindu religion.

The discovery of India's past was complicated by Parliament's
decision in 1835 that Indian subjects be educated in English. India
had been enthusiastically affirmed as a great culture, comparable to
the best that the West could boast. This thought became subjected
to a fresh evaluation by thinkers in England. Under the influence of
Utilitarian philosophy, leaders in Parliament decided that India's past
had not managed to produce anything comparable to what had been
produced in England. Thus, they decided to ignore Indian history and
instead concentrate upon English education for Indians. In the words
of T. B. Macaulay, the secretary for public instruction in 1835, "We
must do our best to form a class who may be interpreters between us
and the millions whom we govern; a class of persons Indian in blood
and colour, but English in taste, in opinions, in morals and in intellect."

The reversal of educational policies had a profound influence upon
both India's appreciation of Hindu religion and European discovery
of it. From that time on, Hindu religion was ignored as a subject of
study by Indians ambitious for promotion in British society. Only
Englishmen with a relentless and stubborn concern about classical
India continued with the task of discovering India. But even they
tended to appreciate India through the spectacles of their previous
education; India was studied in terms of Greek and Latin ideals of

culture. Even today, most Hindu religion presented to the West is tailored to fit the tastes and interests of English-educated people.

THE HINDU SCRIPTURES

The religious literature of Hinduism discovered by British scholars proved to be an impressive but bewildering collection of texts. The Hindu scripture, called "Veda" (Knowledge), is an amalgam of books considered to have been "heard" by ancient seers. The official classification of scripture is *Shruti* (what is heard) over against *Smriti* (what is remembered). Hindus often claim that the texts date from more than five thousand years ago. Outside scholars insist that the best evidence indicates that the texts were in a state of construction from about 1800 B.C. until around 500 B.C. During that time an oral, poetic tradition devoted to hymns of praise to numerous nature gods and spirits changed into a sacrificial system of great exactitude and then changed again into an amazingly esoteric mystical teaching.

The section of *Veda* most fascinating to Westerners has been the last section, called "Upanishad." This series of texts raises profound questions concerning the nature of human life and the ultimate nature of existence itself. The questions raised push speculation to important issues: Why should anything exist at all? Where did things originally come from? For what purpose do things exist as they do?

A puzzling thing about *Veda* is that it seems to advocate a number of different religious styles. The early sections advocate prayers and incantations to various gods of nature—gods of the storms, the sun, fire, and mountains. Later sections advocate a priestly religion requiring elaborate rituals of sacrifice and ceremonies of purification. Yet another section insists that rituals and prayers are "uncertain rafts" upon the ocean of life and that it is necessary for a seeker to renounce the world in favor of a mystical experience found only in isolation.

The variety of religious styles advocated in the scripture represent the variety of religious styles to be found among mankind, say Hindu teachers. Some people in the world are inclined toward a religion of prayer, so the *Veda* teaches the sufficient lessons for these. Some people rise to a concern for priestly religion of ritual and ceremony. The *Veda* also speaks to these. And some rise to a quest for the mystical experiences. The *Veda* meets their needs with the profound teachings of the Upanishad.

A vast body of Hindu literature which does not hold scripture status is called *Smriti* (that which is remembered). It is voluminous—

probably a good deal more than any one person could read in a life-time. Yet the major documents have been translated and are available in English. And some of these texts have become better known than the *Veda* to Westerners. A brief description of a few of these texts appears in the Bibliography.

PRESUPPOSITIONS OF HINDU RELIGION

In order to understand both the appeal and the systematic elab-oration of Hindu doctrines, it is important to know what a Hindu presupposes about the world and man's place in the world. Presup-positions are a part of every religion. They are the unspoken, unde-fended, and assumed ideas which a person within a particular reli-gious tradition holds. Yet these very ideas shape the doctrines which emerge as the public explanation and defense of a religion. Thus they are of fundamental importance when attempting to understand a re-ligion. Believers employ them to interpret reality, whether they realize it or not. They function much like a pair of spectacles which a person might wear: all that a person sees is brought into a particular focus, clarified, or tinted by the spectacles through which he looks. Religious presuppositions are religious spectacles.

In Hindu religion there are three major presuppositions in the structure holding together all doctrines and practices. These presup-positions tend to be shared by Hindus. And as presuppositions, they are not debated, defended, explained, questioned, or even much thought about by the ordinary Hindu. They are assumed to be true; and yet all of life takes on meaning because of them.

A major presupposition which can be traced back to Vedic scrip-ture is the notion that human society is divided into classes. This was institutionalized as the infamous caste system (*varnāshrama*). One Hindu scriptural section insists that when the world was formed, it was created out of a huge manlike being (called *Purusha*). Human society resulted from the dividing up of the huge being.

> When they divided primal man,
> Into how many parts did they divide him?
> What was his mouth? What his arms?
> What are his thighs called? What his feet?

> The Brahmin (priest) was his mouth,
> The arms were made the Prince (*Kshatriya*),
> His thighs were the common people (*Vaishya*),
> And from his feet the serf was born (*Shudra*).

Thus from the very beginning of things, the text says, society has had divisions. The priests (Brahmins) are at the highest level; the military/aristocracy (Kshatriya) class is next; the common people such as merchants and farmers (Vaishya) follow; and at the very bottom is the service class (Shudra). The nature of the world is such that there must be these divisions. They date from the very beginning. People are not equal; nor do people have equal say in how things are to be accomplished politically, militarily, socially, or spiritually. Democratic or egalitarian thinking suggesting "all men are created equal" has no place. From the beginning of things there were these divisions; they are a part of the very structure of reality. To violate such divisions is to attempt to violate the nature of reality. One does not break a law of nature; the law of nature always breaks someone who attempts to violate it.

In Hindu society caste came to be determined by heredity. If a person's father was a priest (Brahmin caste), he too would be a member of the Brahmin caste. If one's father was a servant (Shudra caste), he would be a servant as well. Caste determined occupation, social rank, privileges, responsibilities to the social order, and liabilities. Certain occupations came to be the responsibilities of certain classes of people. Both privilege and liability follow birth into a caste. Numerous rules and regulations spell out for each caste what privileges, responsibilities, duties, and liabilities belong to the particular caste. Daughters inherit caste, too. But marriage within the caste is arranged for the daughter by the parents (and in some cases, even by the caste leaders).

Hindu religion developed an amazingly complex system based upon this presupposition that social divisions are built into the very structure of reality. Caste status was determined by one's parents' status. Intermarriage between caste groups was prohibited. Social interaction among caste groups was kept to a minimum. Elaborate sets of rules concerning pollution and purification developed, particularly among the top three caste groups who generally held themselves aloof both from one another and from the bottom group.

Caste as a presupposition makes certain attitudes inevitable. Members of a particular caste are regarded, in effect, as members of a specific species. The distinction between castes is very much the same distinction as between humans and animals. Humans do not marry animals, nor do they eat or socialize with them on equal terms. As there are different rules or ethics for dealing with animals, so are there different rules or ethics for dealing with different castes.

The consequences of these assumptions is important for the moral life of a Hindu. No universal ethic is drawn up by the religion itself.

A person relates to others simply in terms of *who* they are in the caste system. There are no general principles of moral behavior which one must apply to all people. This line of thinking leads to a measure of toleration and a general acceptance of various moral beliefs and be-haviors. But the toleration is based upon the same principle others might assume when they tolerate differences between animal behavior and human behavior. That is, one does not ordinarily expect a dog or a cat to live by the same moral rules as a human. The differences between humans and animals are too great. A Hindu assumes caste differences are unchangeable as the moral distinctions between a hu-man and an animal.

The caste system is supported by two other presuppositions. These are the ideas of rebirth (*samsāra*) and of the causal law (*karma*). From the scripture emerges the view that people after suffering death are reborn. The human soul reincarnates, or transmigrates, to another body.

The idea of rebirth is not unique to Hindu India. But it does function in Hindu thought as a fundamental assumption. A soul is reborn into another existence after death. When the new life termi-nates, it necessitates yet another birth. An endless chain of lives and deaths occurs. Successive births are not likely to be on the same level of existence. A person may be reborn as a human or as an animal. A person who dies as a Brahmin may be reborn as a Shudra or as an animal.

The life process for an individual dates back to the very beginning of things. And it reaches into the future as well, since transmigration will continue to occur. A soul inhabits a body for its alloted time; then the body dies and the soul moves on to a new body. Thus life is a continuous series of birth and death, birth and death. The terror of death and the trauma of birth are not once-for-all events, but events which repeat themselves over and over and over.

What comfort some might find by thinking that rebirth will occur (thus death does not really end things) is dashed by the causal law (karma). The causal law of karma holds that one's past action deter-mines one's existence. Stating karma in such a succinct way might reduce its significance as a presupposition. Karma is an immovable law which holds always. Every thought, every word, every deed has a future consequence. Moreover, every thought, word, and deed itself has been produced out of previous thoughts, or words, or deeds.

Karma means that a human being is locked into action by the iron law of cause and effect. Past acts determine the present and the future. What a person does now results from past actions, and these present actions will determine future actions.

There are three component aspects to karma which may be detailed to show its comprehensive control of life. There is the aspect of karma which means that some karmic effects have been realized already. That is, one has been born into a certain caste, to certain people, with certain mental and physical abilities or disabilities. All of this is due to past acts. Where, when, how one is born has been caused by karma.

A second aspect of karma is that some past acts have yet to bear their consequences. Deeds done in the past, maybe in previous lives, must and will have consequences. No act escapes the causal law. Thus a person must await the inevitable workings of the law of karma. And one doesn't know whether deeds of the past will bring good fortune or bad.

Yet a third aspect of karma is that deeds done in the future will bear their own particular consequences. What a person does from this point on will have necessary consequences. No deed is exempt.

So the law of karma maintains that human life is locked into a web of causal relations determining both present conditions of life and future events. One never gets away with anything, for every act has a consequence. Moreover, who one is results not from society's ills, not from poverty, race prejudice, sexual gender, or even chance. What a person is follows from what he or she has been in the past. Caste, rebirth, and the causal law all fit nicely together. Social status is the direct result of karma. Rebirth occurs only because the person causes it to occur. And how it occurs is determined by what was done in a previous life.

THE GOAL OF HUMAN LIFE

The implications of *samsāra* and *karma* drive Hindu thinkers toward the inevitable conclusion that life itself is a bondage, a slavery. Human beings are not free. They are bound to the wheel of existence, destined to continue through the endless process of birth and death. After all, the law of cause and effect controls each human life.

Thus what people desire from the depths of their being is freedom. People want to be liberated. They want to experience unhindered existence, to realize a liberation unfettered by karma. Hindu thought, therefore, defines the ordinary human condition as bondage. It insists that the only proper goal of human life is freedom.

Hindus interpret all of human life in these terms of bondage and the human quest for liberation. Since all people are in bondage, they all strive for freedom (whether or not they are aware of such striving). Human behavior is understood as an effort to become free.

According to Hindu thought, human life and human history are not to be explained by theories of a divine purpose in history, by laws of economics, by forces of good and evil. Human history, both personal and collective, is the drive of all beings toward the personal realization of total freedom. All beings are consciously or unconsciously aware of personal bondage. And all beings instinctively act to realize their own freedom. This urge explains the behavior of the scholar, the politician, the artist, the physician, the thief, and the murderer. Each is striving to realize freedom, whether he knows it or not.

Classical Hindu thought is based upon these presuppositions concerning human bondage and the goal of liberation. Western thinkers do well to ponder the significance of this view of the human condition. This general theory of human behavior gives Hinduism a remarkably liberal, unrestrained, and even, anarchic tolerance. All men desire freedom, this view maintains. But not all people are at the same level of development toward an inner sense of what real freedom might be. So people often give themselves to the pursuit of things which provide them with only an immediate or temporary realization of freedom.

Guided by this view, Hindu thought developed four general categories for ordering the variety of human behavior that is seen in the world. These categories of behavior define acceptable boundaries within which to pursue freedom. These categories also provide the means by which to understand what other people are doing.

Some people devote themselves to the pursuit of wealth and power. Almost from the time they are children they are marked by characteristics of gathering, gaining, winning, securing. They seem unconsciously driven to gain and to succeed over others. They are competitive; they strive to profit in their relations with others. They usually profit not only monetarily but administratively and politically. They are convinced, consciously or unconsciously, that their own freedom is enhanced by their acquisition of wealth and power over others. But all of their behavior is driven by the endeavor to escape bondage and to realize freedom.

Other people seek liberation in different ways. Some pursue a life of pleasure. They assume that one realizes an enlargement of the personal self by aesthetic or erotic experiences. The cultured appreciation of good music or art expands the hearer or viewer. Aesthetic experiences pull a person out of himself into a larger domain of sensation. The self is expanded, moved into a realm of beauty, sensation, and emotion which is far more expansive than that which is known to the person who delights only in wealth and power. Hindu thinkers maintained that the pursuit of freedom through aesthetic experience (and its close associate, erotic experience) centers in the emotional life and the disciplines related to refined cultivation of the senses. A vast literature devoted to the arts as expressions of the quest for freedom grew in India from an early period. A vast body of erotic literature grew based upon the assumption that the same attitude a little girl takes toward her teddy bear or a man takes toward a woman he loves is not dissimilar to the expression of feeling in the arts. The secret to both is mastering certain skills of relationship. These skills expand the personal self beyond the confines of isolated existence.

Yet another way in which people pursue liberation is dedicated duty. This is an expression of concern for others as though others were a fundamental extension of oneself. Hindus believed that a person might experience a sense of freedom by expanded concern to other people. One may take the attitude of concern toward anything or anyone (except, of course, a person of another caste). But Hindus concentrated upon certain relationships in their literature devoted to this topic.

A particular relationship which illustrates the mastery of this pursuit is the relationship to be found with a mother and her child. A mother is concerned with her child as a fundamental and indistinguishable part of herself. After all, she carried the child within her as it took life and grew. But a mother cannot and does not relate to her child in the manner of the lover or the aesthete. Rather, she extends herself in loving concern for the child, always ready to give, to forgive, to discipline, to nourish. Yet the mother realizes that she must separate herself from the object of her concern and let the child become an independent adult. The mother masters a relationship of concern without attachment. She loves the child, will do anything for it, but she must finally let the child go. The child becomes independent as it grows. Yet the mother's love and concern remain.

Hindu thought has maintained that mastering this difficult attitude of love without attachment enhances personal freedom. Love and attachment are not the same (however often popular music and cinema equate the two). The attitude of concern expressed properly through devoted duty to others is an expression of the desire for liberation. And freedom is realized to a limited extent.

Yet Hindu thought maintains that there is no final realization of liberation except emancipation from the round of birth and death. This liberation is designated by the terms *moksha* or *mukti* in Sanskrit. Freedom is experienced only partially in the attainment of wealth and power, of aesthetic experience, or of duty. The real goal of life is to be totally and completely free. It is to be released from the bondage of karma and the cycle of birth and death. But it is also to be no longer at the mercy of what is not oneself, to be free from restrictions and constraints, things or persons other than oneself. It is to be able, in short, to do or not to do anything. It is to be unattached, unbound.

FREEDOM AS A GOAL

The Hindu account of the human condition and its goal differs significantly from the dominant tradition of the West. The main tradition of European thought reflects a regular and persisting commitment to some notion of a highest good, a commitment to moral perfection within human limits. This value, promoted by Plato and by early Christian thinkers, both presupposes and teaches a number of things about man which are formative for religious thought in the Western world. The most significant of these formative principles is that human perfection consists in the control of human passions by the intellect and that the reasoned life is the best life. Thus, people are admonished to pursue a balanced life through the discouragement of the appetites and desires to the extent that they would overpower reason. Augustine, Aquinas, Descarte, Locke, Hume, Kant, and even Bertrand Russell (however significant their differences might have been) affirmed this general view that morality is man's highest aim and that we must exercise reason if we pursue it.

There have been dissenters to the dominant tradition of the West. But the main tradition of thought in the West has treated dissenters as dangerous voices. Dissenters questioned the high priority given to morality or to reason. They suggested that high value should be placed upon spontaneity, growth, science, or aesthetics. Among the dissenters one can find William Blake, Meister Eckhart, Jacob Boehme, and Nietzsche. Contemporary Existentialist thinkers such as John Paul Sartre or the "Pop" psychologists advocating "self-realization" over against moral duty or obligation are dissenters as well.

There is no question that the "dissenters" have gained status in the popular mind of recent years. So it is not too surprising to find that Hindu thought has become popular in a society which exalts "value-free" scientific inquiry leading to an enhanced control over human life, that makes man "the measure of all things," or that advocates the pursuit of personal fulfillment and adjustment as ultimate goals.

A major religious text of Hinduism in the modern world (found in virtually every tourist hotel room in India) is the *Bhagavad Gita*. The text (not officially scripture, but a primary text of modern Hinduism) clearly teaches the supremacy of freedom over morality. In the *Gita* the main character Arjuna complains to his counselor Krishna that if he participates in the coming battle against his kinsmen, he will participate as well in the destruction of the very foundation of a moral society. Krishna counters Arjuna's moral considerations by telling him that it is more important for him to be *himself* than to be a cog in the social machine. It is better that he fulfill his capacities as a man of certain gifts. In so doing he will enhance his control, his freedom. He can learn to become master of his circumstances rather than one who is dictated by them. Arjuna's obligation to himself is more important than any obligation to society or to some standards of an absolute morality.

This supremacy of freedom over morality in Hindu thought is clear to anyone who reads the tales of ancient India, who studies *yoga*, or who considers the attributes of the *guru* (wise man) celebrated in Indian texts. Emphasis is placed upon a cagey awareness, an ability to act freely and decisively in complicated situations, and a mastery over oneself and others. The truly wise man is one who is "beyond good and evil."

THE PHILOSOPHICAL STRUCTURE OF HINDU THOUGHT

Hindu thought attempts to show that complete freedom can be realized. The different ways in which people structure their lives, pursuing wealth and power, sex and beauty, family and duty—all these are said to indicate that people possess a sense of bondage from which they are fleeing, wisely or unwisely. Hindu thinkers maintain that realization of final freedom is not available by the mere experience of wealth, power, beauty, or duty, but rather through control, a control both of oneself and of that which is immediately outside of oneself. Thus Hindu religion advocates some startling and surprising disciplines (often too arduous for persons seeking only "self-awareness" or "self-realization"). To be free is to be free from all attachments and dependencies. It is to be free to do what one wishes to do; but it is also to be free from limiting factors around oneself. Attaining such a state is the major preoccupation of Hindu religious thinkers.

Whether the ideal of absolute freedom can be realized by an individual stands as a problem for Hinduism. The question may be stated this way: Is the universe such that freedom of this sort is a possible experience? Since "free" is a word denoting the ability to do or to not do certain things, is it possible for someone to have complete control over himself? In short, is it possible to avoid the law of karma?

If freedom is possible, two necessary facts about the universe must be shown to be true. First, events must be shown to follow a causal pattern of relations. Events in the world cannot be simply random happenings, but instead result from cause-effect relations. And second, it must be shown that certain events, particularly those events which mark our "bondage," are subject to our control. If these two issues are not the case, if they are not true, then freedom cannot be realized by anyone. It would mean that there is no way to establish personal control over oneself or over one's situation in the world. Karma could not be avoided.

Thus doubt in Hindu religious thought generally takes one of two forms. One might be filled with doubt if he became convinced that the universe is one great machine firmly bolted together by determinative (causal) relations. This would mean that all things are linked together by causal processes which allow for no intrusions. A child is born with an inbuilt genetic inheritance which determines together with the environment what is to become of it in the world. The child has no chance to control his own destiny. To think this way (to hold to a Hard Philosophical Determinism) is one form of doubt, since there would be no way to break into the causal chain of events determining a life.

A second form of doubt is to suspect that no events in the universe are causally connected to any other events. This is contrary to the Deterministic form of doubt. It is to suspect that the world is simply a random occurrence of events. People are born; they live; they die. But we can never be sure that one event influences another event in this life and death sequence.

The views of doubt might be illustrated by giving some attention to the problem of cancer as a disease which threatens people in our time. If the occurrence of cancer is linked by causal relations to certain foods or to certain types of behavior, it is then possible to avoid cancer. We can be free from its threat by avoiding those foods or those types of behavior which cause it. The key to freedom from cancer is to be found in the cause-effect relations between something (whatever it might be) and cancer. Avoiding the cause frees one from cancer.

But what if a person is unavoidably linked by causal relations to the cause of cancer? What if there is no way to break the causal connection? Then there would be no way to avoid the cause. If a person finds that he *must* smoke cigarettes (and if cigarette smoking causes cancer), then there is no way to avoid cancer. There is no way to be free from the threat of cancer; it necessarily must happen.

On the other hand, if cancer is not tied to any causal relations, then cancer simply occurs whenever and wherever it will. There is no act of avoidance which will free a person from the threat of its occurrence. Either situation would mean that freedom is not a possible experience.

Doubt in Hindu thought takes these two forms. In order to avoid doubt, Hindu thinkers must show that the universe is such that causal relations between events do produce bondage, but that there is enough openness or looseness in the connecting relations so that a person can do something about that which causes his bondage. This requires that Hindu thinkers construct descriptions of reality that will convince their hearers and readers that bondage can be broken and freedom realized.

Another way to look at the issues produced by the Hindu presuppositions is this. The human condition is one of bondage. Is it possible to avoid the workings of the law of karma? Is the universe such that the law of karma can be avoided? Once the Hindu thinker convinces his audience that karma can be avoided, then he must show that there is a route or a path to tread which will release a person from karma.

The questions themselves set up certain kinds of answers to the human predicament as Hindus understand it. The questions assume that a person needs a map or a route to get from the ordinary condition of life to freedom. The route requires a cosmology, an explanation of the universe that reduces it to a path to freedom. The Hindu thinker is engaged in a speculative quest in which he must show that bondage can be avoided and that freedom can be realized. If these abstract philosophical considerations are kept in mind, much of the alleged inscrutability of Hinduism disappears. One finds a fairly simple, albeit carefully argued, path to freedom presented.

RECOMMENDED READING

Basham, A. L. *The Wonder That Was India*. Grove Press (Evergreen), 1959.

Bharati, Agehananda. *The Ochre Robe. An Autobiography.* Doubleday, 1970.

Lannoy, Richard. *The Speaking Tree*. Oxford University Press, 1975.

Potter, Karl. *Presuppositions of India's Philosophies*. Greenwood Press, 1975.

Chapter 6

THE HINDU SYSTEMS

Ordinary people live in bondage, Hindu religion teaches. In the most general sense bondage is the round of birth and death (transmigration) as determined by the iron law of karma. It is also an inability to face specific challenges posed by life in the world. This inability has been created by genetic endowment and/or the social environment into which one has been dumped. Or bondage might be the crippling grip of certain habits which breed further habits. This ever-extending complex of activities and emotions stunts life and makes one miserable. Yet the essential Hindu teaching is repeated over and over: bondage is the condition of being out of control.

The aim of the Hindu religion is to achieve control. And control is freedom. Specific teachings about how to achieve control differ between Hindu schools of thought. But all schools, ranging from Krishna Consciousness to the esoteric meditative techniques of Transcendental Meditation start at this point. All promise to bring the realization of release from bondage. Regardless of whether Hindus have made the proper diagnosis of the human condition or whether freedom is in fact the proper goal of human existence, this starting point must be well in mind before we can appreciate, understand or confute any Hindu claims.

Major schools of Hindu thought have arisen from these assumptions concerning the human predicament and the escape to freedom. Six schools of thought comprise orthodox Hinduism. A look at three of them will provide a sense of the sweep of Hindu thought over centuries. And how these schools have been promoted in the modern period will be the concern of the next chapter.

Care must be taken to examine arguments both in terms of their soundness and their validity. The soundness of an argument has to do with whether an argument conforms to the way things actually are in the world. The soundness of an argument depends upon its accuracy as to facts. The validity of an argument, on the other hand, refers merely to its logical form. An argument may be valid but unsound.

This distinction is very important. One might argue, for example, that "all people in this room are ten feet tall; Jones is in this room; therefore, Jones is ten feet tall." Such an argument is valid. The conclusion about Jones necessarily follows from the premises. But the soundness of the argument is open to question. It is unlikely that one would find a room full of ten-foot-tall people. Thus an argument that is valid might be unsound. No invalid argument, however, can be sound. All arguments should be examined both for their validity and their soundness.

Many arguments made by Hindu teachers depend upon what traditionally was known as *guruvāda* (knowledge of the teacher). It is often maintained that the statements of a *guru* (teacher) are exempt from analysis. Hindus claim that both the validity and soundness tests are inappropriate because a guru has experienced truth that is beyond ordinary mortals. The guru is thought to know more than the student. Students of religion will do well to test all religious claims for validity and soundness. Any teacher who resists good questions is no genuine teacher. If we seek truth, the search for it should not anger or intimidate anyone.

THE SĀNKHYA-YOGA SYSTEM

The oldest of the Hindu schools of thought is called *Sānkhya*. The term *sankhya* has been helpfully translated as "Distinctionism" by some Western scholars to provide a near English equivalent to the basic claims of the school. The discipline of *yoga* has been closely associated with the school for centuries. The school dates from as early as the second century B.C., but received major exposition only in the third century A.D. by Ishvarakrishna, a proponent of the school.

The Sankhya school provides a cosmology (a map of the universe) that employs a primitive theory of evolution. Their cosmology maintains that all things originated out of two primary elements of reality, matter and spirit, or *prakriti* and *purusha*. The whole of the universe as we know it (everything from shoes to ships) evolved out of the basic material stuff, *prakriti*. Prior to evolution into what things are evolving into today, matter was inert, undifferentiated, quiescent. It was simply a huge, globlike mass of material stuff.

All material stuff was composed of three elements or strands in a state of balanced suspension. These three strands are called *gunas* by Sankhya thinkers. The gunas maintained a suspended state for an indefinite period, until something happened to disturb the suspension. Once disturbed, the gunas began to act and the material glob became unbalanced. The activity of the gunas started movement, and that started the change and evolution of material things. According to the Sankhya teaching, the whole of the material universe evolved and continues to evolve out of this primal skewing of the original suspension of the gunas.

Human beings result from the marring of the original suspension of matter. Human beings emerge from gunas acting upon one another. Humans are just part of the cosmic process of matter. And, since it is man's predicament which the cosmology wants to explain (and not the evolution of nature), Sankhya gives considerable attention to the evolution of the human person.

The first important aspect of the human to evolve is consciousness. A further working of gunas upon gunas produces ego (a sense of individuality; separateness). Then evolves mind, then intellect, and finally the sense faculties. The sense organs of touch, taste, sight, sound and smell make people aware of things existing outside the mind. Human beings thus are said to result from the gunas acting upon gunas. Each individual human being is part of the cosmic process which began some time ago and which will continue as a process because the essential elements of matter became unbalanced.

The most obvious parts of a human are material. Consciousness, ego, mind, intellect are all of the same essential nature as the sense organs—they are material. We might think that the consciousness, mind and intellect are immaterial, but the Sankhya teaching claims these are merely different forms of matter.

The human being is tied to the world of evolving matter. Each person becomes a person as part of a determined, evolutionary process. An individual does not come about by his own choosing nor by the choosing of others. All behavior, all thoughts, all inclinations, all emotions result from matter acting upon matter. No man chooses his thoughts; they are the material process of matter acting. No man chooses his actions; they too are determined for him by the movements of matter acting upon matter.

The other element of primary reality is *purusha* (spirit). It does not evolve or act. It does not change. It is entirely passive. There are many of these spirits, one for each being that evolves. And the spirit is the real self of every individual being.

The spirit resides apart from the material body, from the mind, the intellect, and the sense organs. It is free from the workings of matter, it is isolated, and it is an observer. But it does not act.

Human bondage, according to Sankhya, results from confusion about what the real self might be. People confuse mental activity with the passive witness, the real self, the spirit. The mind is material, a part of gunas acting as gunas act. The mind flits from one idea to another as it is forced to by the activity of gunas which make up its essential nature. It can do nothing else.

But humans confuse mental activity with the spirit, the real self. And to do so reduces a person to the activities of matter. People in bondage tie themselves to mind and body. They identify with their mind, in some cases. Or they identify with their body, in other cases. People tend to immerse themselves in the work of the material world and fall under the dominance of the laws of material evolution. This ties them to the processes of old age, disease, death, sorrow, disappointment, pain, and suffering.

Yet, Sankhya maintains, each person has a real self, a spirit, that exists free from the material world. A person can realize this free self as isolated. The theory attempts to show how to bring about such a realization of the self.

The normal process required to bring about realization of the self is the practice of *yoga,* which is a "binding" or a "union." Its aim is to bring a person to a realization of the real self which exists isolated and free from the work of matter.

Yoga is an ancient discipline based upon the Sankhya theory of the universe. As such it is not simply a superior form of gymnastic exercise which might promise a slimmer abdomen or greater agility. Nor is it a technique for relaxation from the cares of this busy world. It is, in fact, an occult doctrine. Many of the texts on yoga promise attainment of supernormal powers. And to most Hindu teachers, yoga is not a fit subject for discussion with foreigners or curious dabblers.

Yoga requires through its disciplines a complete reversal of the normal bodily functions in order to bring about a return to the state of original suspension. Its aim is to return the material body (including of course, sense faculties, intellect, mind, ego, consciousness) to a state of suspension. This will enable the discrimination of the real self existing isolated and independent of matter.

Yoga exercises include cleansing the body, controlling breath, and actually reversing normal body processes. The point is to force a person to withdraw from identification with the material aspect of the body. It is to pull identification from sense organs, from the intellect, the ego, the mind, the consciousness inward to bring a sense of union with spirit.

Control of body processes is but the first step in yoga. Postures forcing the body to turn into itself initiate the disciplines. Control of breath and circulation follow. Finally there occurs a state of suspended animation. Breathing seems to stop; the heart remains quiet; the sensations of an external world cease. A yogi enters a trance state marking the first step of realization. An ancient text says, "As a dancer desists from dancing, having exhibited herself to the audience, so does *prakriti* (matter) desist, having exhibited itself to the *purusha* (self)."

A second path to realization of the real self is considerably less rigorous than yoga. It appears as a recommended method in the text called *Bhagavad Gita*. This method is literally a concession to the fact that not everyone has the requisite mental or physical discipline to embark upon the rigors of yoga. It is called *karmayoga*.

The karmayoga method has been taught to many Westerners thought to be mesmerized by materialism. It advocates a studied practice of indifference to material events. The key to karmayoga is to act in the world as one finds that he must, but to act without thought for the consequences of the actions. A basic statement of the discipline makes it appear simple: "Act without attachment to the fruits of your acts." But it requires that a person learn to separate himself from what it is he is doing.

Acting without attachment means to dissociate oneself at all times from consequences of acts. While a person acts in the world, he must do things, but he need not identify with the results of what he does. It means that a student would act as a student, would study with diligence, would produce what a student must produce for assignments. But the student would not identify himself with the consequences of study, whether those consequences might be grades, a job, a reputation, or an honor. One does what he must do. But he separates himself from the results.

Most people appreciate this notion of disinterested action. There are occasions when one finds it necessary to be forebearing or gracious simply for the sake of being so, not for any reward. It is the proper thing to do. Moreover, most people disrespect artists who paint pictures merely for money or athletes who compete only for material gain. But the *Gita* extends this ideal of disinterest because it is teaching that the real self is unattached and isolated from all that occurs in the material world. The self is lodged in a body. But the body must learn that there is a fundamental distinction between it and the real self. What the body does is of no concern to the real self. Human action in the world is of no moral or spiritual significance to the real self. It is the nature of lightning to flash. Lightning *is* the flashing. Even so it is the nature of a body to act. It is no different from its function. But the real self is isolated, unconnected, free from the acts.

Practitioners of karmayoga promise that gradually the disciplines of nonattachment produce an inner sense of separation from the world. A realization dawns that one is not dependent upon matter or material things. Awareness of a real self existing independent from the body and free from its entanglements occurs. A sense of freedom and liberation breaks.

THE SHORTCOMINGS OF SANKHYA-YOGA

From within the Hindu religion Sankhya has been subjected to considerable criticism. The case for Sankhya rests upon a series of inferences which Ishvarakrishna develops in the *Sānkhyakarikās,* 2nd century A.D. He contends that since human life is anxiety-ridden, there must be a state of tranquillity and peace. Moreover, since anxiety is produced by the change inherent to the material world (people grow old, suffer weaknesses, diseases, frustrations), there must be a spiritual world of permanence and nonaction.

Some Hindu thinkers attacked these arguments as being invalid. Ishvarakrishna's conclusions do not necessarily follow from his premises. One might conclude from his premises that human existence is a meaningless process of birth and death.

But the major attack on the Sankhya cosmology emerges from considering the soundness of the theory as a path to release. The theory is supposed to describe reality in such a way as to provide a means to release. Fundamental questions, however, must be raised about its description of the human predicament. Does Ishvarakrishna adequately account for the confusion between matter and spirit which is said to take place? Normally people confuse only similar things, things of a similar nature. Rarely, if ever, do people confuse dissimilar things (I never confuse round with square or white with black). Yet matter and spirit are confused, it is said, thus bondage results. How is it that evolving, changing, acting matter is confused with quiescent, nonacting, isolated, free spirit? How can such dissimilar things be confused? If the cause of such confusion cannot be explained, what then of the soundness of the description of the human predicament?

A second level of criticism is even more troubling. Can liberation even be achieved by thinking of the world in the *sankhya* manner? How can an act of the mind (part of matter) or of the will (part of matter) or of consciousness (part of matter) put a person in touch with spirit? At what point is there a link or connection between matter and spirit which might allow a person to experience spirit?

How can anything done on the material level of reality bring about an experience unrelated to it?

The second criticism is most troubling for Sankhya thinkers. It suggests that they have not properly described the human condition of bondage. Moreover, if they cannot provide a correct diagnosis of the problem, the proposed cure must be questioned. And if they cannot show there is a connection between bondage and freedom, then they cannot assure release. One must be able to pass from bondage to matter to a dimension of liberation of the spirit. But unless a specific connection between the two can be shown, there is no assurance that any human act might save.

THE ADVAITA ALTERNATIVE

The best known Hindu school of thought emerges as an alternative to the shortcomings of the Sankhya school. Its Sanskrit name is *Advaita*, meaning "nondual." It bases its teaching upon the Upanishad texts of the *Veda* and is sometimes called *Vedanta*, meaning "end of the Veda." So sometimes it is called the Advaita Vedanta School of Hindu thought. The primary texts date from as early as the sixth century B.C., but systematic development of the school culminates with the work of India's most famous philosopher, Shankara, in the ninth century A.D.

The *Advaita* alternative to the Sankhya theory rests upon a very simple assertion. There is actually only *one* reality, the reality of Spirit. There is one Spirit, and it is the only reality. Everything else that gives the impression of being a substantial and independent reality results from a bewitchment of the mind. In short, the world of ships, shoes and sealing wax is an illusion.

The Sankhya thinker meets difficulties in trying to relate the material world to the spiritual world; the advaita thinker avoids these problems by stating that the material world simply does not exist. It is not real. It is but an illusion.

The Advaita teaching is stated in this short assertion: there is a complete identity between the real self (called *ātman*) and the one power sustaining the cosmos (*Brahman*). In short, Ātman is *Brahman*. The real "me," the "I" that is prior to any thoughts about "me," the thinker that does the thinking in any thought process, this real self is identical to the ultimate reality.

But whence comes this sense of an external world which we all seem to share? How is it that we are so certain that a world of ships, shoes, sealing wax and other things exist. Why does it appear that there are many different things in the world, including many different people? Why am I not immediately aware of my oneness with ulti-mate reality?

Advaita thinkers provide the answers to these questions by appeal to human error and ignorance (*avidya*). We think that the world exists because we project upon the world out there characteristics and prop-erties which it does not in fact have. Just as when someone walks through a forest in twilight and mistakes a coiled rope in the path for a snake, so do people project wrong characteristics upon the world. The rope did not design the illusion of a snake. It is but a rope. A person makes the mistake. People attribute to a place where they do not exist nor belong a whole world of ships, shoes, sealing wax, and many other things. The problem is with us, people. We make the fundamental mistake of ignorance and we construct an imaginative world of things. But they are unreal, illusory, false.

In the same way that we might get over the illusion that the rope is a snake, we can get over the illusion that the world is real. We must attack the problem from the side of the creator of the illusion, that is, from our side of the problem. Both the problem and the so-lution lie with us.

Ignorance can be overcome by knowledge. Just as a flashlight reveals a "snake" to be nothing but a coiled rope, so the light of truth shows that we have taken something for real that is not real.

The issue of how people superimpose reality upon that which is not real is a fundamental concern of Vedantist thinkers. The issue has to do with providing a correct description of our problem, namely, ignorance. Because only a correct description of the human problem will provide means to avoid doubt, the issue of superimposition is crucial. How is it that we impose over reality that which is not reality?

The ancient arguments and the modern arguments differ. The ancient thinkers were concerned to question our tendency to think of the world as made up of separate, independently existing things. So the ancient thinkers raised epistemological questions—questions dealing with how we know what we think we know. Modern argu-ments concentrate primarily upon how we mistakenly impose value upon things in the world which have no value.

The ancient arguments about superimposition are of this sort: When we claim to know one thing over against another thing, we name the properties of the thing we know. If we identify one person over against other people, we name the person's properties, such as hair color, eyes, body size, skin color, etc. But a thing's properties are not the real thing itself, Hindu thinkers remind us. A person's hair color, eyes, or body size are not really the person. These things are all properties, not the person (one might shave all hair, one might gain or lose weight, one's eye color might even change). The person is something other than specific properties. Thus what we appeal to when we distinguish one thing from another cannot really distinguish one thing from another. But, then, what does distinguish one thing from another, one person from another? Advaita thinkers would answer, "Nothing!" We have simply superimposed, projected, distinctions upon things and persons. What we have taken for truly distinguishing characteristics are not. Nothing distinguishes one thing from another. All is one, they insist.

A modern version of this sort of argumentation provides a critique of contemporary culture. People and society superimpose value upon things which by themselves possess no value. A new automobile has no real value (no intrinsic value). We impose value upon it; we make it valuable; and we make one more valuable than another. Clothes have no intrinsic value to them. We impose importance upon them. If we lived in another time or another place, we would see that the particular style we value now is an artificial and relative distinction imposed by us. Our form of government, our way of doing things, our preferences, our distinctions are all relative and even arbitrary. We put value upon things, ideas, styles, ways of living. But the value is artificial. It is relative. It is not lasting. It is not real. The things themselves have no claim to value apart from what we project upon them.

The modern Vedantist thinker wishes to remind people that any culture is simply the superimposition of value upon what is fundamentally without real value. What is real lies much deeper. It has to do with what is ultimately real and not with a passing phase or an artificially imposed significance which is here today and gone tomorrow.

Most people prefer to live as though these illusions were real. They continue to put value upon wealth, upon fame, upon possessions, as though there were something intrinsically valuable in these things themselves. They end up frustrated, disillusioned, embittered, and fooled because they live in a culture which has superimposed phony value upon things which carry no value.

So modern Vedantist thinking varies a bit from the traditional teaching. Whereas the older teaching launched a comprehensive attack upon "certain" knowledge of an external world, modern Vedantism concentrates upon cultural criticism. In this sense Vedanta contributes significantly to what has been called the "counterculture" movement of recent times.

The older teaching may be illustrated by one of the numerous anecdotes to be found in Hindu lore. A king once sat at the feet of the famous philosopher Shankara to learn. But the king resisted when Shankara told him to regard all things, including his exercise of power and the enjoyment of his wealth, as no more than a projection of false reality upon what is actually real. When the king was told that the one and only self which is the ultimate reality merely *seems* to be multiple because of his ignorance, he decided to test his teacher.

The following day when the philosopher came to deliver his usual lecture to the king, a large, dangerous elephant, maddened by heat, was set loose to charge the philosopher. Shankara turned and fled, climbing a tree with surprising agility for a philosopher. When the elephant was subdued, the king approached the philosopher and inquired, "Why did you flee if the elephant was but an illusion?"

Shankara replied with the composure only a philosopher could muster, "Indeed, the elephant is non-real. Nevertheless, you and I are as non-real as the elephant. Only your ignorance made you see a non-real me climb up a non-real tree."

Modern Vedantism addresses itself to issues more suitable to contemporary society. It raises questions concerning the soundness of commitments and preoccupations in a world of artificially manufactured reality. A glance at the works of artists, novelists, songwriters, and filmmakers indicates a general mood of disenchantment which Vedanta thinkers exploit. In fact, some of the lyrics of popular music, particularly of the 1960s and 1970s, reflect criticism of the complacent ease and smugness of a society Vedanta adherents for some time had termed superficial. Paul Simon sang about a society in which "the people bowed down and prayed to the neon gods they made," and Pete Seeger with others sings about Americans content to live in "little boxes on the hillside, little boxes made of ticky-tacky, little boxes . . . all the same." And Carly Simon writes a critique of even the counterculture movement when she suggests in "Playing Possom" that everybody caves in to the false comforts of society at some point.

> We lived up in Cambridge
> And browsed in the hippest newstands
> Then we started our own newspaper
> Gave the truth about Uncle Sam
> We loved to be so radical
> But like a ragged love affair
> Some became disenchanted
> And some of us just got scared.

Then you moved to the country
Bought a farm and tilled the land
Then you took your books to India
And got hooked on a holy man
But the wells they do run dry
And the speeches turn to words
And the woods are full of tigers
And freedom's for the birds.

Now you run a bookstore
And you've taken on a wife
You wear patches on your elbows
And you live an easy life
But are you finally satisfied?
Is it what you were lookin' for?
Or does it sneak up on you
That there might be something more?[1]

Such criticism noting the restless movement from cause to cause until finally there is a collapse into the prevailing value system is even more pointedly stated by adherents of Vedantism such as Aldous Huxley, Gerald Heard, or Christopher Isherwood. But the success of the pop artists implies that criticism of modern materialism registers with many people in contemporary society. Some might charge that these words themselves are but superficial tittle-tattle, designed to generate material profit. The fact that they are taken seriously by masses of people ready to put down money for records suggests that there is a soundness to the cultural criticism they carry.

AN ALTERNATIVE TO VEDANTA

Despite Vedanta's pertinence as a device for culture criticism in the modern world, it has long been subjected to serious examination regarding its own claims. Vedanta alleges that human bondage is not really a material bondage (as Sankhya maintained) but is rather an epistemological (belief-related) or spiritual problem. It is epistemological because bondage results from ignorance, incorrect knowledge. It is spiritual because people have been seduced into belief and confidence in materialistic concerns and materialistic solutions to life's problems. Yet the material world is an illusion. To think of it as real is to make a mistake. To base life upon the illusion is to suffer spiritual distress.

---

[1]Copyright by C'est Music ASCAP. All rights reserved.

By denying reality to matter, the Vedantists avoid the problem which skewered the Sankhya thinkers. Their solution raises another problem. The new problem is both epistemological and spiritual. What causes the false sense of a material world? How is it that we are so certain that the world of material things is real? Why do we seem to be experiencing a world of many things if the world is but one vast spirit? From where does this ignorance come?

And even more problematic for the Advaita thinker are questions such as these: If the world is but one vast spirit, why do we share the ignorant conclusion that it is made up of many things? Where did this conclusion come from? What is its cause? Who is ignorant? Who makes the mistake? Is Brahman (ultimate reality) making the mistake? Is it being said that the one vast spirit has made a mental error by suggesting to me that I am an individual? Has Brahman erred? How could what is described as ultimate "intelligence" make a mistake?

These questions and more force a suspicion that the soundness of the *Advaita* arguments is doubtful. More doubt enters the inquiring mind when procedures for realization of the truth are examined. If the world as we know it is an illusion, and if bondage is ignorance of that, what kind of a causal relation exists between bondage and freedom? A relation between what is said not to exist and what does exist is no relation at all; it is verbal confusion. There can be no causal relation between nothing and something. Yet Advaita thinkers persist in maintaining that something you or I do while operating in this illusory world will bring realization of the real world. But how can anything done in an illusory dream world have an effect upon the real world? What sense is made of either human bondage or freedom with this sort of talk? It seems that no good sense is made of either. The human predicament has not been adequately characterized; nor has the route to liberation been rationally described.

Advaita thinkers are hopelessly stuck at this point. They are forced to endow the material world with enough reality to assure their listeners that something done in this illusory world will make a difference in realizing what is real. But if they say that the material world has some reality to it, then they bring back all of the intellectual problems which skewered the Sankhya.

Problems with the intellectual consistency of the Advaita teaching, no doubt, is one reason why modern Advaita thinkers avoid calling into question the actual existence of the material world, but instead raise questions about the materialist values of the Western world. But there is nothing uniquely Hindu about such criticism.

Even a cursory reading of Christianity's New Testament provides a sustained criticism of materialism. One can only conclude that the appeal of Advaita is less rational than emotional. The trenchant criticism of Western culture appeals to any who are disaffected or disillusioned by life in a highly competitive marketplace of commerce and ideas. Debunking such a society is far easier than a sustained, rational objection to the goals of society.

THE QUALIFIED NONDUALIST ALTERNATIVE

Some Hindu thinkers abandoned the nondual assertions and constructed instead a theistic system which avoids the epistemological problems inherent to the Advaita by uniting matter and spirit under God. This view holds that God (Brahman, Ulitmate Reality) chose to evolve or emanate into the world by manifesting himself as spirits and then as material reality. Brahman is ultimate reality. Out of Brahman emerge spirits (*Purusha*). And out of the emergence of spirits comes matter (*Prakriti*).

But Brahman (God) embraces all three levels of reality. He is manifesting himself in different ways as spirit and as matter. He is both the same as and different from the things of this world (the same, because he is the essence of all; different, because he is one, but the world is many). All things evolve out of Brahman.

The system is called "Qualified Nondualism" (*Visistadvaita*) and dates from the eleventh century A.D. The main thinker associated with this cosmology is a man named Ramanuja. It is a patently theistic cosmology, though it is important to remember that its implications are pantheistic—God pervades everything. God, says Ramanuja, is the First Cause, the First Mover, the One Power, and also the Essence of reality.

Ramanuja offers strong objections to the Advaita view. He argues that the Advaita assertions rest upon a fictitious foundation of altogether hollow and vicious arguments. For example, Advaitans argue that since we know objects only by an awareness of properties and that properties are never the essence of a thing itself, therefore, we have no knowledge of separate things and must conclude that all things are essentially the same: Ramanuja insists that all objects are characterized by properties. There are no things devoid of properties. Hence we cannot prove that there is any reality apart from properties we experience. By the Advaita argument, we would have no reason to believe that Brahman exists either. Thus the argument is hollow; it asserts nothing significant.

Moreover, Ramanuja argues that for Shankara (the leading ex-ponent of Advaita) to engage in argument is to assume what he him-self wants to deny. For him to argue is to take differences seriously. Thus he assumes differences to be real. Yet he also wants to say reality is one and without any differences. He assumes what he denies and then denies what he has assumed. Again, the Advaita argument is hollow, asserting nothing.

Finally, Ramanuja insists that the theory is vicious because it cannot and does not promise deliverance, liberation. To do anything about ignorance, to do away with it, we must know its cause. But what is the cause of our ignorance? We cannot say that the individual self is the cause, for the sense of an individual self is itself caused by ignorance. We cannot say that Brahman is the cause of ignorance because Brahman is defined as intelligence. So the argument is vicious. It seduces any careful thinker into despair and doubt.

So, Ramanuja says, the nondualist thinkers are wrong. Instead, Brahman is the One Power who evolves as Spirit and Matter which we experience as the world. Spirit and Matter are both real. And they are related to one another by Spirit being the cause of Matter.

Brahman (God) carries an essential nature of infinite knowledge, blessedness, joy, bliss. This essential nature constitutes the inner self of all that evolves in the world. Our individual selves are but various modes of the manifestation of Brahman. Yet the true nature of these selves is obscured by ignorance, and thus we are in bondage because we do not know that we are literally one with God. Freedom is the intuitive realization of the individual self as one with Brahman. The material world has come about because Brahman engages in sport and bestows bodies on individual spirits and enters into them and ani-mates them. Thus the whole world emanates from Brahman.

Release is the realization of the spirit's freedom from the material body. It is literally a release from the body, since any body lives con-fined to a realm of space, time, and causality. A body can be in only one place at a time. A body can exist at only one time frame (no body can exist at two times at once). And all bodies are subject to the laws of cause and effect. Thus anyone who thinks of himself primarily as a body and lives according to its limits is in bondage. There is a spirit within, however, which is one with ultimate reality. Realization of the "spirit," the real self within, brings about a liberation from the confines of the material, bodily world.

The Qualified Nondualist cosmology is assumed by every modern Hindu theist. Difference among the sects of Hinduism varies with regard to questions like these: Who is the ultimate being? Who is

God? What is His name? How is He to be addressed? Three major sects of Hinduism exist today, the worshipers of Vishnu, the worshipers of Shiva, and the worshipers of the Mother Goddess. Each is organized with a sectarian bureaucracy, with priests, and with rituals of initiation and control. Sectarian differences are sometimes sharp enough to cause misunderstandings and occasional debates among devotees of the various sects.

A surprising latitude exists among Hindu theists, an amazing tolerance. The cosmology itself favors tolerance since it suggests that ultimate reality manifests itself into the world in various ways. Thus any god worshiped by people might be a manifestation of Brahman. After all, he is the essence of all reality, it is said.

The International Society for Krishna Consciousness (ISKCON) is presently the most visible witness of Hindu theism in the Western world. Krishna devotees hold that Krishna is the manifested name of Brahman, that he has shown himself in the world numerous times, and that he is the underlying energy of all material reality. Yet Krishna is spirit. He is the First Cause, the Prime Mover, he is the One Power behind all that occurs in the world. What happens in the world is for Krishna's entertainment, it is said. Krishna engages in sport when things occur—presidential elections in the United States and terrorist acts in the Mideast are all a part of Krishna's sport. And all is done to draw individual souls back to a realization of their oneness with Krishna. Thus, an individual needs to renounce attachment to the material world and "get in touch" with the underlying energy of Krishna that vibrates forth into the world. ISKCON recommends a ritualized chanting as a means to establish vital contact with the ultimate energy which brings the mind and spirit into harmony with Krishna Consciousness.

The Qualified Nondualist cosmology provides Hindus with an amazingly adaptable, flexible, almost elastic theology. It can be stretched to imply a compatibility with some Christian teachings. It has had an appeal to some Muslims in India. And it is used in various ways to promote Hinduism as a spiritual base for life in the modern scientific and technological world of Western Europe and America. We will show the elasticity of Hinduism by giving attention to modern varieties of Hindu thought in the next chapter.

RECOMMENDED READING

Dasgupta, Surendranath. *A History of Indian Philosophy.* 5 volumes, Motilal Banarsidass, 1975.

71903

Potter, Karl. *Presuppositions of India's Philosophies.* Greenwood Press, 1975.

Zaehner, R. C. *Hindu and Muslim Mysticism.* Schocken Books, 1969.

Zimmer, Heinrich. *Philosophies of India.* Edited by Joseph Campbell. Princeton University Press, 1974.

Chapter 7

THE NEW FACE OF HINDUISM

India's history during the last two centuries has profoundly molded contemporary Hinduism as most people in the West might experience it. Englishmen traveled to India not to colonize but to exploit India for trade. In time England embraced India as part of the Common-wealth of nations gathered under the Crown, ruling her for 200 years.

The factor which had the greatest impact on Hinduism was the English education of Indians. English education exposed an elite of Indians to a set of ideas and values which implicitly called into question the ideas and values of traditional India. They formed a class who would serve as interpreters between the British and the Indian masses. They became the "Intelligentsia," straddling two cultural worlds and attempting to connect them by discovering some linking ideas.

Indians became Englishmen not only in a political sense, but as part of a strategy to "create a class of people, Indian in blood and colour, but English in taste, in opinions, in intellect, and in morals." The pros and cons of British imperial strategies are the subject of numerous scholarly pieces. But it is difficult to overestimate the im-pact of imperialism on Hindu religion.

Any Hindu member of the Intelligentsia was faced with formi-dable questions: Is there any value to traditional Hindu thought? Does Hindu religion have anything to say to the modern world, to wealthy and powerful Englishmen? Is there anything at all a Hindu can say to those who consider India a barbaric, degrading, and heathen country? Can some essence of Hindu culture be retained even though political and social pressures demand changes? Is there a *practical* value to Hindu religion, or is it an archaic system of beliefs having no significance whatsoever to the forces of modern living?

Modern Hindu thinkers confronted questions such as these. In doing so they constructed a "Neo-Hinduism," the preferred philoso-phy of a surprising number of people today.

The case for Hinduism was forcefully presented in the late nine-teenth century by a most unlikely person—one who cared or knew little about the problem of British rule and seemed to care little about the decline of Hindu culture. Moreover, he was not a member of that class created by the British to be interpreters of British social prin-ciples to the masses. In fact, he received little or no formal education in either English or Sanskrit, but remained content with his native and regional Bengali language.

His name was Gadadhar Chatterji. He was born in 1835 in rural simplicity. At age six he began to have visions of Kali (the mother goddess in her horrific form, often associated with disease, death and destruction). The visions frightened him, but following the visions he often experienced a peace and tranquillity which impressed his con-cerned parents. His elder brother took him to Calcutta at age sixteen, where the two of them were installed as priests of a new temple on the Hooghly River, a branch of the Ganges. The temple was built to honor the goddess Kali, and the young priest directed his devotional energies toward cultivating her favor.

Young Chatterji's devotion was extraordinary. Trance often ac-companied his worship, and his trances attracted attention because of their frequency and their intensity. A physician examining him during a trance could detect no trace of a heartbeat. Yet the young priest always returned to normal consciousness, astounding his lis-teners with tales of conversations with gods and goddesses.

As a priest, he took the name Ramakrishna Paramahamsa. And as his fame grew, he experimented with other sects of Hinduism and with other religions. He considered God to be manifest in various ways and various forms. God showed himself as the divine mother (Sita, Durga, Kali), as Rama, the epic hero, as Krishna, as Vishnu, as Shiva. But Ramakrishna maintained that God also showed himself through Muhammad, through Jesus, and through the prophets of Is-rael. He took instruction from Muslim and Christian teachers and managed to have visions of the Christ Child and of Mary, the mother of Jesus. Muslim and Christian mystical experiences seemed to occur for him as easily as mystical experiences of one of the Hindu gods or goddesses.

Ramakrishna's religious virtuosity attracted considerable atten-tion. He began to teach a fundamental unity of all religions, based on his religious experiences. Various religious doctrines are nothing more than human opinions, he maintained. Statements made by religious texts and teachers bear no significant authority whatsoever. He illus-trated his views by numerous homey, yet insightful stories and max-ims.

Even as there are many paths up a mountain, only one summit is reached.

You may take your cake with icing either straight or sideways. It will taste sweet either way.

Even as many streams unite when merged into the ocean, so do many religious points of view join when ultimate truth is experienced.

Ramakrishna's point was that religion does not really deal with doctrines, arguments, and propositions. Religion is *experience*. It is not knowing something (as in knowing geography or mathematics). Rather, it is experiencing something. In one of his talks Ramakrishna compared religious experience with religious knowledge. It is as though a person were to enter an orchard filled with fruitbearing trees. A person might begin to speculate about how many trees there might be and the productive capacity of such an orchard. Or a person might walk into the orchard and pick a piece of fruit and enjoy the orchard for what it is. Ramakrishna warns that there are some who wish to make religion into a commercial venture. Others occupy themselves with endless analysis and disputation about doctrines and beliefs. But some realize what religion actually is, he says. It is the experience of mystical bliss and joy. Thus, the claims of Hindu religion over against the claims of Christian or Muslim religion are issues to be set aside. There is no point to any discussion of them. Moreover, the relation of ancient Hindu religious statements to modern scientific theories are equally pointless. Experience of God is the point of religion. To do anything else with religion is to make a mistake. And the wise person will realize this, said Ramakrishna.

Ramakrishna's experimental saintliness did not go unnoticed among young Indians. Some thought him to be a fraud. They presumed their education in modern thought provided adequate means to debunk and expose Hinduism, a relic of ancient India. Among the critics of Ramakrishna was Narendranath Datta. Born to an aristocratic Kshatriya family of Calcutta, Datta early came under the rationalistic and scientific thought then current at the English schools. He read widely in European science, liberal economic theory, and democratic political thought. Mill, Kant, Hegel—all figured in his college reading program. He even corresponded with Herbert Spencer.

Datta's first encounter with Ramakrishna troubled him. He went to the temple grounds to hear Ramakrishna and to debate with the priest. He left profoundly impressed. When he returned for a second visit, Ramakrishna singled him out for special attention. Accounts of the "special attention" differ. One account claims that Ramakrishna merely touched Datta with his foot and Datta fell into a trance in which he saw the things around him merging together into one undifferentiated reality. Ramakrishna, seeing Datta's terror, laughed and told him, "Let it go for now." And all returned to normal for the young student.

Datta became a close disciple of Ramakrishna. When Ramakrishna died in 1886, Datta took the vow of a monk, changed his name to Vivekananda, and embarked upon the customary pilgrimage through India's sacred territories. When he returned he organized and headed the Ramakrishna Mission.

Vivekananda was unlike Ramakrishna in many ways. In the first place, he was educated according to the English system. And during his pilgrimage time, he found himself troubled by India's grinding poverty, her social backwardness, her mental inertia. Yet he also recognized a cultural wealth which India possessed. He meditated before great monuments built in former times, and he pondered writings of India's great thinkers of the past. His conclusion: India was not bankrupt and totally dependent upon England and the nations of the West. Rather, Western nations needed India. But they did not need her for economic gain. Rather, India possessed a spiritual legacy which she could share with others. India, he maintained, could provide a spiritual base for modern life.

Vivekananda's thought drew inspiration from Ramakrishna. But he extended Ramakrishna's mysticism into a criticism of modern life in Western nations. He proposed a renewal of spiritual life in Europe and America, guided by Hinduism. As a critique and as a proposal for spiritual renewal, Vivekananda's thought is fundamental to modern Hindu religions. One hears his expansive interpretation of Hinduism over and over when Hindu religion is preached to Europeans and Americans.

VIVEKANANDA'S HINDUISM

In 1893 Vivekananda appeared unexpectedly at the World Parliament of Religions, meeting in Chicago. Without official invitation or status, he attracted considerable attention by wearing traditional Indian clothes to the sessions. He gained access to a seat on the conference platform, and one day addressed the assembled delegates. The *Chicago Tribune* printed parts of his talk which chided delegates for their "imperialist" attitudes toward Eastern religions.

> We who come from the East have sat here on the platform day after day and have been told in a patronizing way that we ought to

accept Christianity because Christian nations are the most prosperous. We look about us and see England, the most prosperous Christian nation in the world, with her foot on the neck of 250,000,000
Asiatics. We look back into history and see that the prosperity of
Christian Europe began with Spain. Spain's prosperity began with
the invasion of Mexico. Christianity wins its prosperity by cutting
the throats of its fellowmen. At such a price the Hindu will not have
prosperity. I have sat here today and I have heard the height of in-
tolerance. I have heard the creeds of the Moslems applauded when
today the Moslem sword is carrying destruction into India. Blood
and sword are not for the Hindu, whose religion is based on the laws
of love.[1]

Vivekananda's words shocked Parliament delegates. But they listened and supported efforts to have him address audiences at major
universities in America and Europe. What Vivekananda presented
in his lectures and brief writing is a creative synthesis of traditional
Hindu ideas and modern scientific and democratic thought. Like most
creative geniuses, he did not bother with details of Hinduism or with
complexities of modern thought. Instead, he mined Hindu tradition
and modern scientific thought sufficiently to construct an expansive
and unspecific appreciation of Hinduism and science. Many take his
work to be the creation of a "Neo-Hinduism"—a religion which is
remarkably uncritical and naive. At the same time it is sentimental
in its appeal to a *vocabulary* of traditional Hinduism. An unspecific
"Hinduism" and an unspecific "science" appear over and over in
Vivekananda's work. Any who take the time to read or listen to
contemporary Hindu missionaries will encounter Vivekananda's "Neo-
Hinduism."

Vivekananda employed the language of the Qualified Nondualism
cosmology (see Chapter 6 for explanation of Qualified Nondualism)
and made use of its distinctions concerning matter and spirit, reality
and illusion, at the same time as he maintained that there is a god
who rules the world. But Vivekananda was not concerned about
reconciling traditional Hindu school thinkers or systems. Rather, he
wanted to show that Hindu religion is capable of absorbing and spir-
itualizing the intellectual movements of modernity which many
thought were undermining Christianity.

Vivekananda was aware that the threat of Darwinian evolutionary theory was not so much its claim to explain the world without
recourse to a deity, but that it claimed to explain life by the principle
of natural selection. Such a principle seemed to imply that progress

---

[1]*Chicago Tribune,* 20 September 1893.

in the world occurs through competition, by survival of the fit, by *lassez-faire* principles of economics, by militarism and strength. In the minds of many, Darwin's theory seemed to justify racism, militarism, and imperialism. The Social Darwinist rhetoric maintained that the strong white nations possessed a natural right to rule less developed nations.

Vivekananda countered the Darwinian theory by suggesting that Darwin and his cohorts left out the most important element in evolution, namely God. The biological theory is a conclusion reached by examining only one sort of data. Hindu philosophers for centuries talked of evolution, Vivekananda maintained. The absolute Brahman manifests itself in the world by evolving into the multiplicities of the universe. He sends the world outward from himself. But he brings it back into himself. The process is one of involution and evolution. Scientists record only the slow movement of material nature back toward its origins in the Absolute. Mankind, too, is involved in this pull of all things toward the Absolute Brahman.

Hindu thought spiritualizes the evolutionary theory, Vivekananda maintained. Without the spiritual dimension of Hinduism, evolutionary theory leaves only the teaching that "might makes right," the "survival of the fittest," a rationale for militarism, racism, imperialism, and warfare. These things are natural, good, and necessary for progress in light of the scientific theory. But the Hindu concept of God added to the scientific theory eliminates the negative implications of evolution.

> When you see man as God, everything, even the tiger will be welcome. Whatever comes to you is but the Lord, the Eternal, the Blessed One, appearing to us in various forms, as our father and mother, and friend, and child; they are our own soul playing with us. . . .

Vivekananda insisted that the ancient Hindu view of the world and Darwin's theory are compatible. Both posit evolution. But Hinduism spiritualizes it, avoiding the unethical social implications of the biological theory.

Vivekananda also addressed relativity. Though the work of Einstein and Heisenberg appeared somewhat later, Vivekananda was aware that both physicists and historians were concerned about the implications of relativity. Physicists were reminded daily of the uncertainty of perception and knowledge: What we see and value under certain conditions we do not see and value under other conditions. Historians were impressed by how much the modern world differed from the ancient world: Ptolemy's theories might have been sufficient for the questions of his time, but were quite irrelevant and insufficient for any modern theory of the universe. Historians faced a troubling question. Does "historical consciousness"—the awareness that the past was qualitatively and quantitatively different from the present— mean that every traditional idea and practice must be constantly reex-amined?

Vivekananda mined Hindu religious thought to find evidence that the problem of relativity was not a new one for Hindu thinkers. He turned to the ancient term *maya;* illusion. Hindu thinkers coined this word when they became convinced that the world of matter is false, a superimposition of human imaginings upon the one great spiritual reality. Vivekananda insisted, however, that *maya* need not refer sim-ply to illusion. He believes it refers to the tendency of human beings to settle for mistaken ideas about reality.

> *Maya* does not mean "illusion" if "illusion" is taken to be the opposite of reality. *Maya* indicates the relative reality of the world and of human life. The world is an indefinable mixture of reality and appearance, of certainty and illusion.

Hindu thinkers have long asserted that the world does not in itself tell us what to make of it, argued Vivekananda. The world does not spell out a morality for us. We make mistakes all of the time in de-ciding what to do with our knowledge of the world. Mixing oxygen and hydrogen might produce a glass of cool, refreshing water. But the same two elements can also be combined to make a blowpipe feed a destructive flame. What to do with our knowledge is always a prob-lem. So relativity is no new issue for Hindu thinkers.

A third matter of concern to Western religion was the First Law of Motion. Galileo posited and Newton mathematically formulated this law which says that no force is required to keep an object moving with a uniform velocity in space. A body continues indefinitely in its state of motion or rest unless some force acts upon it. This law enabled astronomers to explain the movement of planets without appealing to some supernatural forces of spirits or angels as the movers and directors.

The First Law of Motion explained a lot for astronomers. But it also troubled many thinkers. Aristotelian mechanics had insisted that for every moving thing there had to be a mover (something to start it moving). Aristotle's principle of motion made possible a neatly constructed logical argument showing that there must finally be a Prime Mover in the universe—that is, there must be a God. But the scientific mechanics removed the Aristotelian arguments for the existence of God from "intelligent" discussion.

Vivekananda argued that the modern scientific First Law of Motion is simply a restatement of what Hindu thinkers had said for centuries: All things in the universe are struggling for liberation. The universe is a whirl of objects striving to realize freedom. Only the force exerted by other things, gravity, prevents the universe from exploding outward into infinity.

> The whole universe embodies a striving for freedom. The earth is trying to fly away from the sun, and the moon from the earth. Everything has a tendency to infinite dispersion. All that we see in the world has for its basis this struggle for freedom. It is under this impulse that the saint prays and the robber robs.

Science confirms the Hindu view of things, Vivekananda argued. Even nonliving objects ache for liberation. We can apply scientific law to social deviants (the robber steals because he wants to be free), to religious devotees (saints pray and undergo austerities because they want freedom), and to all things in the universe by combining Hindu spirituality with modern science.

And finally, Vivekananda synthesized Hindu religion and modern democratic political theory. The major flaw of English, French, and American democratic theory is that they base themselves upon a conception of human rights. The democratic nations of the West insist that all people equally have the natural human right of life, liberty, and the pursuit of happiness.

The problem with the Western foundations of democracy is that placing human rights as the base for a democratic state puts each man in competition with each other man. Thus, a person cannot realize his natural rights unless he asserts himself against other people who are attempting to realize their natural rights at the same time. Freedom and self-fulfillment within the democratic sphere is achieved only by each person aggressively asserting himself against everyone else. Competition and struggle become the handmaid of democracy. People get what is due them only by taking from others.

Hindu thought sees all men as equal manifestations of divinity, Vivekananda insisted. Each person is a manifestation of divinity in the world. Therefore, Hindus do not consider asserting rights over against rights. Rather, a person need only recognize the divine individuality of other people. The emphasis upon individuality is important: All are equal manifestations of God. But not everyone has an equal or identical function within a society. Some function best in a capacity of leadership. Others function best as intellectuals. Still others excel in a commercial setting. And others find their individuality best realized in serving others. Each is fulfilled as an individual when doing what comes naturally, when doing "his own thing."

Vivekananda argued that the ancient caste system of Hinduism laid a better foundation for a democratic organization of society than the theories generated by European and American thinkers. Vivekananda agreed that the ancient system of caste suffered corruption over the centuries (it became wrongly tied to clan, family, privilege, and heredity). But the ancient insight behind the system of caste was that a society requires four groups of people to function smoothly: administrators, intellectuals, businessmen, and service people. Society must be structured so that each person can find what it is that he does well and naturally. Then that person can move into the sphere where he works best. In doing so, each person finds fulfillment without competing with others or hurting others.

VIVEKANANDA'S LEGACY EXTENDED

Vivekananda died in 1902. The Ramakrishna Mission which he fostered and led in India continues today as a monastic organization dedicated to Vivekananda's interpretation of the meaning of Hindu faith and of Ramakrishna's significance. The mission engages in some social work and in educational service to India.

Vivekananda's legacy to the Western world was the establishment of the Vedanta Society, which today maintains branches in major cities of the United States and Western Europe. The Vedanta societies attract a significant number of people who feel a disenchantment with Judeo-Christian institutions. The society's dominant effort is to provide people with reminders of the spiritual dimension of modern life and techniques for discovering that dimension.

In India however, Vivekananda's thought was extended through Aurobindo Ghose. The son of an Indian physician in Bengal, Aurobindo grew up under English influence and when seven years old was sent to England with his two brothers to gain a "proper" education. Until age 21 Aurobindo remained in England studying European languages and literature. He failed his Civil Service examination on a technicality and was excluded from the service of the British government in India. Aurobindo returned to India as a teacher and principal of a private college in western India. There he studied Indian languages and history, and by 1904 had moved to Calcutta to take a leadership role in the Indian nationalist movement.

Aurobindo played a central role in the fight to oust the British from India until 1908 when he was arrested and jailed on charges of complicity in a bombing incident. Aurobindo's efforts in nationalist agitation had consisted primarily in editing an underground news-paper dedicated to the nationalist movement.

In his newspaper work Aurobindo made much of the cosmology which Vivekananda had employed to discuss science and political theory. Aurobindo extended Vivekananda's thoughts to show that Hindu thought supported the nationalist revolutionary efforts. Au-robindo reached back to the ancient text *Bhagavad Gita* and its main character Arjuna to show that the Hindu goal of *mokṣha* (liberation) required first *swaraj* (self-rule). But self-rule at a personal level was impossible without self-rule for the nation. He maintained that a revolution to overthrow the British rulers was a prerequisite to any spiritual goal the Hindu religion might preach.

The text *Bhagavad Gita* served as a model for Aurobindo in his call for militant activity. The text is based on a consideration of war. It depicts Arjuna as troubled about his role as a soldier. Arjuna did not want to engage in violence and killing. But Krishna, his counselor and advisor, shows him by repeated arguments that final liberation will come to him only by allowing his body to do what it is that this body is capable of doing best (yet without attaching himself to his acts).

Aurobindo insisted that even as Arjuna was given a vision to see that all events moved inevitably toward the battle which he faced, so the sensitive Hindu must see that the events of British rule and its suppression of the Indian people were but events forcing the rightful revolt and rebellion of the Indian people.

India's destiny is to be free. Suppression is but an occasion for India's resurgence as a free people. To act militantly to express free-dom is to practice karmayoga. Aurobindo maintained that he expe-rienced a vision of Krishna while imprisoned by the British.

> He placed the *Gita* in my hands. I was not only to understand intellectually but to realize what Sri Krishna demanded of Arjuna and what he demands of those who aspire to do His work, to be free from repulsion and desire, to do work for Him without demand for fruit, to renounce self-will and become a passive instrument in His hands, to have an equal heart for high and low, friend and opponent, success and failure, yet not to do his work negligently. I realized what the Hindu religion meant. . . .[2]

---

[2]Uttarpara Speech

Aurobindo applied the teaching of karmayoga to the revolutionary effort. The particular body a person has is simply the body which results from acts done in previous lives. Its tasks, inclinations, capacities and abilities are there because of karma. The body, then, acts according to the conditions in which karma places it. Lightning is no different from its flash (lightning is what it does; it is the flashing), so the body is no different from its function in the world that has been determined by karma. A person realizes freedom by letting the body do what it is designed to do.

The ethical implications of this teaching are problematic, to say the least. Yet, consider the conditions of British rule. They praised democracy, but denied it for the Indians. The activities for freedom might be justifiable even apart from Aurobindo's curious teaching. Those who read his frequent calls for revolution easily forget that Aurobindo advocated passive resistance against the British.

Few Westerners find the Gita's teaching morally acceptable. Traditional Western ethics assume that a person is free and morally obligated to choose between alternatives of right and wrong, good and evil. To choose not to choose is still to choose. The Gita's teaching as presented by Aurobindo suggests that moral deliberation concerning human acts is irrelevant and unnecessary.

Aurobindo managed to win acquittal in the trial dealing with his alleged involvement in the bombing incident. After acquittal he retired from nationalist work and moved to the south of India where he settled in the French protectorate of Pondicherry. There he devoted himself to extensive writing, to the establishment of a monastic community, and to laying plans for an international utopian community based upon his theories of human development.

Aurobindo began to examine human life in terms of Vivekananda's thoughts of reconciling science and religion. He attempted to show the meaning of the cosmic process as it applies to mankind. In this effort Aurobindo extended even further the boundaries of modern Hinduism.

Involution is prior to evolution, according to Aurobindo. The Absolute, the Godhead, pours itself into the world to make the world. But the purpose of the plunge into matter is to return to itself again. Matter is therefore not a contradiction of spiritual consciousness; it is simply the lowest expression of it.

Divine consciousness practically wipes itself out in the process of transforming itself into inert elements which make up the physical world. Matter grows into more elaborate organizations of particles joining to form atoms. Atoms form inorganic molecules. Inorganic molecules combine into living cells and multicellular units. All of this shows the Absolute pulling the divine consciousness back toward itself.

The whole process is infused with the divine pull toward a final spiritual realization involving everything. The evolutionary process is one of movement from inert matter to organic life to vital life and then to the realm of mind. Mind appears first as intuition. Later, intellect (the capacity for discrimination and analysis) appears. The next step is toward realization of a Supermind, a realization of divinity.

We live now at the level of mind expressed through intellect. Through applied reason, we are producing a technological wonderland. But there is another step. It is the step to a realization of the Supermind, a level above mere intellect. Attainment of the Supermind will bring a psychic and spiritual transformation comparable in scope and significance to the change from mere organic life to intellectual life.

According to Aurobindo, the scientific theory of evolution misses the important issue of involution. And in missing involution it misses the spiritual significance of the whole process. Scientific theories of evolution propose an aimless process without purpose or meaning. The theory of involution sees first the descent of God into matter and matter evolving only for the purpose of realizing its own latent possibilities. When the divine consciousness reaches its furthest limits, it swings around again and once more climbs the steps. Evolution, then, is a growth toward realization of the divine essence within all things.

Technological advances result from the mind expressing itself through material things. The making of amazing drugs, the development of computers to solve problems in a fraction of the time a human mind might do them, engineering feats that have men walking in space, and surgical procedures undreamed of but a few years ago are all produced by the intellect integrating itself with previous levels of evolution. Each advance makes use of ideas and procedures developed at a lower level.

But even as evolution began at some distant time and level of materialization, no reason exists that it must end with the present level of mind and intellect. Aurobindo maintained that the next step is evolution to the Supermind. And such a step will bring about a transformation of humanity into gnostic beings, into supermen.

It is important to take note of the baggage a person takes along on this speculative excursion with Aurobindo. First, Aurobindo is assuming that all change in the world is progress, advance. All change moves us toward a greater integration of things, a higher mode of being. Second, he assumes that such progress is inevitably determined by a cosmic process initiated and powered by God. It continues because all things tend to become more complex at the same time as they integrate with a lower level of development. The process is cosmic, and it is divine. The Absolute, the Divine, moves out of pure spirituality into matter and back toward itself again.

The soundness of such teaching is open to question. Where would we look to confirm such assertions? Are we asked to believe these things on faith? And, if so, why?

Moreover, does change to complexity necessarily imply progress? Is there any reason to believe that the *quality* of life today is any better than it was one hundred, two hundred, or three hundred years ago?

Aurobindo naively claims that technological advance implies moral and spiritual advance. But where is there evidence for such a view? In fact, a look at environmental decay, exhaustion of finite natural resources, and the threat of a nuclear holocaust imply quite the opposite conclusion from Aurobindo's.

Furthermore, Aurobindo's thinking assumes that change in the organization of matter implies change in moral values as well. But this is to say that there can be no absolute moral values because all things are changing, evolving. A particular moral value or moral rule represents only a particular perspective offered by a particular time at a particular level of evolution. At one period of time what is seen to be an ideal society is at some later time considered to be barbarous and evil. Good and evil are relative.

Finally, we should note that this theory says the technological thinking that has produced the present society with its terrors and its opportunities is a necessary consequence of evolution. There is no way to stop this sort of thinking and development; nor is there any good reason to want it stopped. Technology promises us a new society. But the new society will force people to adopt a new morality based upon ideas more advanced than the archaic notions of individuality, personal freedom and selfhood that produced the old morality.

But while Aurobindo did not publicly go so far as to say that all technology is good and that all things in the world are "peachy," a reader looks in vain for any principles which might bring ethics into play. Aurobindo's readers are left with encouragement to look for what is "best" in mental development (though how to define "best" or "good"—the most important issue of ethical thought—is left unattended). In fact, a curious and cagey self-interest creeps into Aurobindo's writings: We are forced to conclude that the "evil" of British imperialism in India was actually a "good" which caused Indians to move toward a higher realization of political freedom. Such a moral shell game leaves everyone guessing about right and wrong and provides no guidelines for moral choice.

Theories of evolution and some troubling technological developments threaten the religious and moral limits of human thought. Aurobindo's scheme is a creative effort to resolve these dilemmas. But a failure to include an ethic short of "might makes right" or "if it can be done then do it" is frightening in its naïvete. His scheme takes the principle of "doing your own thing" to its ludicrous but ominous limits. Because someone finds himself with both an inclination and a talent for lying, cheating or stealing does not imply that he ought to do such things. But Aurobindo's teaching suggests just that—with the only limiting proviso being that one should act "without attachment" in doing such things. After all, Arjuna's battle against his kinsmen turned out as no Sunday school picnic on the grass; it was a bloody horror.

Yet the foundations for modern Hindu thought are laid by these men: Ramakrishna, Vivekananda, and Aurobindo. The foundation provides for a grand extension of traditional Hindu thought; and it alleges to be compatible with modern scientific thought. But the new boundaries of Hinduism make it compatible with only the most superficial assessment of science.

The new Hinduism encourages a search within oneself to achieve harmony with the forces of change in the modern world. The inner search is attractive to many today. To fall into "the flow of things," to "get into touch with the processes of growth," to sense a harmony with a divine energy which works beneath the more visible forces of change in the world is an inviting alternative to struggling with moral choices. And it is especially appealing to those who are troubled by a sense of incompetence before the impersonal institutions which manipulate us. Caving in to the pressures for conformity and going with the flow is far easier than finding good reasons to take a stand at some position of moral obligation.

Various Hindu movements in America offer but a gloss on the ideas of these three Hindu thinkers. Transcendental Meditation advocates looking within by means of a meditation technique. But it provides no advice concerning how to live in this world. Its followers claim advantages ranging from amplified sexual powers to uncanny skills at winning at the stock market.

Krishna Consciousness devotees maintain closer ties to an authentically Indian heritage by dress and lifestyle. They teach that through prayer and rhythmic chanting a person can achieve contact with the divine energy underlying the material world. And all the Hindu movements emphasize the cosmic process which is working itself out in the world. The call is to conform to the process, to "get in touch" or to "tune in" and not to worry.

But the process of "getting in touch" threatens to stunt the will, to make it nonessential and subordinate to the teaching, the teacher, or to the alleged process of development. Flowing in the current of things without the mechanism of the will, without the means to choose, is to abolish even the occasion for morality. Morality requires the conscious choice among alternative courses of action. Counsel to "accept the flow" is counsel to abandon moral consciousness.

RECOMMENDED READING

Hutchins, Francis G. *The Illusion of Permanence*. British Imperialism in India. Princeton University Press, 1967.

Johnson, David L. *The Religious Roots of Indian Nationalism*. Firma K. L. Mukhopadhyay, 1974.

Religion and Change in Contemporary Asia. Edited by Robert F. Spencer. The University of Minnesota Press, 1971.

Religion in Modern India. Edited by Robert D. Baird. Monohar, 1981.

Shils, Edward. *The Intellectual Between Tradition and Modernity: The Indian Situation*. Mouton, 1961.

Chapter 8

BUDDHIST RELIGION

Buddhism began with one man, Siddhartha Gautama, and he lived in the sixth century B.C. The Sanskrit/Pali term "Buddha" (Awake, Enlightened) was applied to him because he and his followers believed he had "awakened" to the reality of things, while ordinary people lived in a daze of sleepiness and ignorance.

Attempts to reconstruct the actual life of Buddha are fruitless. Only a rough outline can be given. He was born about 563 B.C. to a family whose patriarch was probably a feudal lord (living not far from the modern Indian city called Varanasi). His full name was Siddhartha Gautama of the Shakya clan. Siddhartha was his given name; Gautama, his surname; and Shakya designated his clan affiliation as well as his caste standing in the increasingly complicated Hindu social system.

Siddhartha lived a comfortable life by the standards of his day. Legends make it difficult to know just how comfortable his life was since there is a tendency to exaggerate the luxury of his early life in order to emphasize the magnitude of his renunciation. Despite his easy life, in his middle twenties he became profoundly discontent. Though married and the father of a young son, and heir to considerable wealth and power, and enjoying all the comforts available to the wealthy of his time, Siddhartha was unhappy.

The background of his discontent is contained in the legend called "The Four Passing Sights." According to this story, Siddhartha's father consulted fortunetellers prior to Siddhartha's birth. They agreed that the child to be born was unusual. His career in the world might go in one of two directions. He might take a path in life which would result in his holding great political power. Or he might choose a path which would make him not a king but a great spiritual leader.

Siddhartha's father, the legend maintains, determined that he would see his son rise to *political* power. Once the boy was born, he spared no effort to keep his son's mind attached to the concerns of the world. The pleasures made available to the young Siddhartha, legend holds, would be enticing to any youth: forty thousand dancing girls, three palaces, horses, education, sport, wealth. Moreover, troubling issues about life were kept from the boy by a strategy of sending men to clear the roads of any offending sight whenever Siddhartha was away from one of his palaces.

However, one day an old man was overlooked in the road-clearing efforts. Siddhartha met an old, decrepit, broken, trembling, weak human being. That day Siddhartha confronted old age. And it troubled him.

On another day, Siddhartha encountered a person lying on the ground racked with painful sickness. And on a third day Siddhartha encountered a funeral procession in which a corpse was carried followed by weeping, grieving family and friends.

The three passing sights of old age, disease, and death troubled Siddhartha. On a fourth day he saw among a crowd of people a man who had renounced the world of material comforts, a man with a shaved head, a simple robe, and a begging bowl.

A deeply troubled Siddhartha contemplated the four passing sights. And the stories agree that in a short while Siddhartha discovered that the objects which had earlier brought pleasure could no longer satisfy him. He determined to leave the snare of pleasure constructed by his father, to renounce the world, and to seek liberation from old age, disease, and death.

The four passing sights had convinced Siddhartha that satisfaction and fulfillment in life do not come through the enjoyment of material things. Possessions, family, power, and pleasure cannot make life complete. Siddhartha determined to search for fulfillment through renunciation and self-denial. One night when he was twenty-eight, he left his wife, his young son, and his estate. Mounting his great white horse, he rode off alone into the forest. There he shaved his head, abandoned his fine clothing and horse, and began his search for liberation through self-denial.

He joined a group of severe ascetics who taught that the *body* prevents spiritual fulfillment. The body's dependence upon food, clothing, and shelter ties it to the world. Thus, liberation from suffering cannot be found unless one can achieve independence from this dependency. So Siddhartha practiced independence from material things. He fasted to show independence from the need for food; he lived outdoors to show independence from the need for shelter; he avoided clothing and cleaniness to practice independence from conventional social values. In his yoga exercises, he attempted to stop respiration and circulation. Siddhartha's body could not tolerate such stress, and he fainted from starvation and ill health.

The failure of severe austerities to bring release from old age, disease, and death convinced Siddhartha that self-denial cannot bring liberation. Austerity had only made him older, weaker, and sicker—even to the point of death itself. Rather than releasing him from the problem he saw, self-denial had only pushed him toward the problem. So Siddhartha concluded that there must be a middle way toward release, a middle way between self-indulgence and self-denial. He had experienced both. But neither brought release from disappointment, failure, frustration, and sorrow.

Turning his back upon mortification of the body, Siddhartha found his companions in self-denial turning their backs upon him. Alone now in his search, Siddhartha devoted himself to his own discipline of meditation and thought. One evening, the stories say, near Gaya in north India, as Siddhartha was sitting beneath a pilpul tree, he experienced enlightenment.

The stories of Buddha's enlightenment meet no critical test of authenticity. Māra, the spirit of the world of sensual pleasure, called his demon hosts to attack him with whirlwind, tempest, flood, and earthquake. But Siddhartha was not frightened. Māra then tried seducing him with his three beautiful daughters: Desire, Pleasure, and Passion. But Siddhartha remained unmoved. It is said that for some forty-nine days Siddhartha endured the onslaughts of hosts of gods and spirits and demons—some encouraging him, others, such as Māra, trying to frighten or dissuade him.

At the dawning of the forty-ninth day, Siddhartha discovered the truth concerning the cause of suffering and unhappiness of all kinds; and he realized what a man must do to overcome suffering and unhappiness. Siddhartha's inner change was so profound that he decided to return to the stream of life and trudge the dusty paths of India to tell others about his discovery. In time Siddhartha established an order of monks who shared his conviction, and he attracted hundreds and thousands of lay followers.

THE TEACHING OF THE BUDDHA

The texts say that shortly after his enlightenment, Gautama searched for his former companions to tell them of his success. He found some of them at the Deer Park near Benares (modern Varanasi).

Buddha's message to his former companions lays down four propositions which testify to his discovery. This, his first sermon, carries the kernel of early Buddhist teaching about liberation from life's sorrows. The brevity of his propositions suggests that over the centuries these statements have been honed to a formula. Nevertheless, the Four Noble Truths (as they are called) constitute the core of Buddhist teaching.

The first of the Four Noble Truths is that *human life is suffering*; it is illness; it is misery. Buddhist scriptures repeat this assertion over and over in various ways. In one rendering, Buddha explains the proposition by saying:

> The world of transmigration, my disciples, has its beginning in eternity. No origin can be perceived, from which beings start, and hampered by ignorance, fettered by craving, we stray and wander. A mother's death, a daughter's death, loss of kinsmen, loss of property, sickness, all these have you endured through long ages—and while you felt these losses and strayed and wandered on this long journey, grieving, weeping because you were bound to what you hated and separated from what you loved, the tears that you shed are more than the water in the four oceans.[1]

This negative assessment of human life is fundamental to the Buddhist teaching. The evils mentioned are central to the life process—sickness, old age, death, as well as dissatisfaction with the conditions of life.

Texts do not deny that people might be able to have some fun. However, human enjoyment occurs at a superficial level—a level suitable for animals who can enjoy and forget, but unsuitable for the human being.

Buddha's conviction about this truth is summed up in a famous story about a grief-stricken woman who appeared one day with the request that Buddha restore her dead infant to life. Buddha agreed to do so when the woman returned to him with only one mustard seed from a household which does not know death. The woman hurried to search for such a seed. But no matter how far she searched, she could not find one. She returned to the Buddha having learned a central lesson in his teaching: Restoring her infant to life would only be postponing the inevitable. In the life process death continually tears people from one another. To be human is to suffer such pain.

The second truth isolates the cause of human suffering. The cause of suffering, according to the Buddha, is lust, desire, craving. But it is no casual notion of lust, desire, or craving which Buddha has in mind. The desire which causes life's suffering is *the quest for private*

---

[1]Samyutta Nikaya

fulfillment. Every person desires, lusts after, even craves private fulfillment. Each person wants fulfillment as an individual. In order to achieve this fulfillment, each person turns within, separates himself from others, and builds up walls of resistance to protect the sense of selfhood with its private hopes, dreams, and ambitions. Intense selfishness causes all human miseries, Buddha maintained. And it is a characteristic of every human.

Some have suggested that Buddha's insight concerning the second truth can be easily illustrated by handing any group of people a photograph of them taken together. Each person automatically looks for himself first. No one looks first to see the group as a whole. Nor does any look first for a friend. Each looks first for himself. The tendency of human life is to pull away from others, to isolate oneself, to pursue separateness as a means to private fulfillment. Buddha insists that this is the cause of human misery.

The third truth was Buddha's great insight to release. He said, if a person wishes to destroy or eliminate some condition, he need simply eliminate its cause. The insight is simple, so simple in fact, that it is easily missed. To eliminate human misery one need only find its necessary cause. If the necessary cause is destroyed, the condition which is its effect disappears.

The fourth truth spoken by the Buddha in his first sermon is the path for the elimination of the cause of human suffering. It is called the "Noble Eightfold Path" and consists of eight practical steps toward eliminating the sense of selfhood, the craving for fulfillment, and the lust for self-realization. One must acquire proper knowledge, resolve, speech, livelihood, effort, mindfulness, and meditation.

Practicing the Eightfold Path, however, requires that a person abandon ordinary social living and join the monastic community which Buddha established for those sincere in their quest for liberation. Everyone who joined the monastic community had to choose the radical course of leaving family, friends, and vocation to live a life of homeless wandering. Ordinary life is structured to encourage acquiring things, attachment to people, and the necessities of family life; commitment to Buddha's teaching requires a separation from such things.

Buddha was not content that people simply hear his words. In fact, he noted in one sermon that the human situation is as critical as a person wounded by a poisoned arrow. Death occurs unless the arrow is removed at once. It is foolish for the wounded one to inquire: "Who shot me? What did he look like? Where does he live? What sort of family produced him?" The arrow must be removed by drastic and radical action without delay. Even so, a person who hears the teaching of Buddha about the nature of human existence must act immediately. It is foolish to spend time discussing theoretical questions about causes and effects, conditions and events, rights and dependencies. Something is wrong with human life as ordinarily lived, and the cure needs to be applied immediately.

The practical achievement of the Buddha was the establishment of the *Sangha,* an order of monks which exists today. A member of the Sangha is called a *bhikkhu,* or a beggar. A person who chooses to act upon the message must renounce family, occupation, and the world to live the life of a homeless wanderer who begs for his daily bread. This renunciation is for the purpose of experiencing something higher and better than can be found in ordinary life.

But Buddha did not establish anything new to his time. Records indicate that it was customary for earnest young men to leave family and social responsibilities in search of something better. Buddha's order is unique, for it has survived endless debates and attacks in various countries and times. A remnant of the Sangha exists even today in Communist China, despite years of persistent ideological warfare carried on against it by the government. The long history of survival suggests that changes in governments and economies have little to do with the forces which pull men toward a commitment to the ideals of the Sangha.

DOCTRINAL FOUNDATIONS OF BUDDHISM

Buddhist thought provides a curious prism through which to see the world. Taken singly the doctrines provide a fairly straightforward and uncomplicated description of the world in which we live. Yet when assembled as a worldview—a pair of spectacles through which to see the world, if you will—Buddhist doctrine yields some peculiar and troubling conclusions about the world.

Buddhism's basic ideas emerge from the cultural milieu of ancient India. And they include the ideas of *samsāra* and *karma,* the concepts that life is an eternal circle of birth and death, rebirth and death again; and that the cycle of living and dying at various levels of existence is controlled by the law that every act is tied to every other act by the law of cause and effect. Basic Buddhist thinking assumes the ordinary human condition to be one of bondage to the causal law which claims, by implication, that no one is ever free or undetermined in his actions. The ordinary human being is not in control, unfree. The law of karma operates as a universal, immutable law. A person is what he is and does what he does because of previous acts in this life or in previous lives. Moreover, what he will become is determined by the unfree acts presently being done. Human life as ordinarily lived is a life of cosmic slavery to the iron law of cause and effect. (This is illustrated in a previous chapter on Hindu thought; thus what is given here is a general review of what was stated more extensively earlier.)

Buddhists spell out three aspects of the iron law of karma which show its total control over life. First, people experience the karma which has already produced its effects. What a person is now, what he hopes, desires, aims toward, and possesses as capacities and abilities—all these are determined by karma, by what took place in the past.

Second, there is the sort of karma which is yet to bear its effects. Every act done in the past *must,* according to the law, bear some effect. No act is without a consequence. Therefore, everything which a person did in the past must produce something, either immediately or eventually.

Third, there is karma which is yet to accrue. Acts done from this moment on will have their effects to be experienced in some way. Karma is a comprehensive law which covers every aspect of life.

Thus Buddhists begin with certain doctrinal presuppositions shared with Hindus. However, Buddhists add ideas quite contrary to Hindu assertions.

The first doctrine held by Buddhists is the doctrine of *Impermanence (anicca,* Pali)—all things are impermanent. The scriptural formula states, "All things are composite and impermanent"; that is, everything is made up of parts—even atomic particles, ultimately. We never see the essence of a thing itself, we see but a gathering together in one area parts of a thing. And all of the parts are in a state of constant change.

The doctrine maintains that when we see a tree we see color, wood, branches, leaves, a trunk, all arranged in a particular way. We have learned to call what we see a "tree." The parts (or properties) of the tree, however, are all changing. They are impermanent, and the whole thing is impermanent, too.

Let's consider a second example, a town we may call Henderson. "Town" is a name given to a certain sort of configuration of people and buildings. The people and the buildings such as schools, businesses, industries, etc., are all in flux—they are changing. Yet the name of the town, Henderson, stays the same and gives a sense of stability and sameness to that which is actually changing. Should a person leave the town of Henderson even for a month, when he returns he will be surprised to see the change which has taken place in his absence. But a person living within the town is caught up in the change, and thus does not notice it much at all. The person staying in Henderson would, in fact, be participating in the change, would be a part of what is changing.

Buddhists maintain that human existence is painful because people generally ignore impermanence. People know that things change, but they are unaware or they choose to ignore it. One aid for keeping the blinders on is our shared language which reinforces a sense of permanence. People give names to one another and things. These names do not change, though the people and the things change. The names are artificial, but the changing things and people are real. Yet a false sense of permanence is provided by names, by language.

Buddhists hold that reality is actually a series of discrete, separate events. Language and shared expectations and attitudes provide a false sense of permanence. Early Buddhists used the firestick to illustrate the illusion of permanence created by wrong thinking. If a man puts fire to a stick at night and whirls it in a circle in the air, he creates an image of a complete circle of flame. Yet the circle of flame is false. There is only one stick whirling rapidly.

Consider a modern example, motion pictures. Separate celluloid photographs are pulled rapidly through a machine which projects the photographs on a screen in rapid sequence. The visual impression is of a world much like the world we experience. Yet if we slow the machine and examine what is really on film, we see that the image on the screen is very different from what is on the strip of film. Buddhists insist that if we were to slow down our perceptions of the world as we would slow down a film, we would notice that all is changing, all is impermanent.

What we *actually* experience when we experience the world are only properties of things in a constant state of change. We name these properties when we see them gathered together in one place for a time, like the individual people living together and working together in a certain vicinity we call Henderson. But the town Henderson is only a name, a convenient label, used to designate a group of ever-changing elements located in a particular time and place. For Buddhists, all things can and must be analyzed in the same way that one could analyze Henderson.

A second doctrine follows, the doctrine of no self. Impermanence is so complete and extensive that there is no permanent essence to anything. Generally the doctrine is stated as "there is no self" (*anatta*, Pali). But it means that there is no permanent, stable, persisting essence to anything. All things are formed of distinct parts. And all things are changing.

As the doctrine applies to human beings it means that none of us has a personal self which remains permanent throughout the course of our life. All the parts that make up a human person are changing, even the organs by which such change is perceived. Thus, in spite of the fact that we all have a name and some distinct, even peculiar form, there is no essential self behind the body, the mind, the consciousness, the perceptions or the feelings which constitute the human personality. In fact, Buddhist teaching says that what constitutes human personhood are these things brought together in one place: feelings, consciousness, perception, thoughts, body. They are gathered in a particular time and place. But no separate thing called a self or a soul exists to center them or to order them.

This doctrine, strange though it may appear, is central to Buddhist thinking. It asserts by implication that the human predicament of selfishness and suffering results from a fundamental error in human thinking. People ignorantly assume that there is some real self, some soul, to which a name has been attached from birth, and that this exists as something distinct apart from all the changing elements constituting personhood. We know our bodies change over time, our minds change, our feelings change, our thoughts and perceptions change. Yet, we assume that *something* has remained the same. Many people devote themselves to getting and saving and getting more. All the while they are building up mental and emotional walls to protect a self which does not really exist. For this reason, Buddhists say life is painful, disappointing and frustrating.

But, what is personhood? What is it that we refer to when referring to another or even to ourselves?

"A good question," is the typical Buddhist response. When denying the ordinary conviction that there is a self resident in the body somewhere, Buddhists regularly turn to an ancient text called *Milindapanha, the Questions of King Milinda*. In the text a discussion takes place about whether or not there is a "real" self to anything, whether or not there are essences to things. A monk named Nagasena, the protagonist in the text, argues that just as a chariot cannot be identified as essentially wheels, or chassis, or spokes, or axles, or seats upon which people ride, neither can a person be identified with any one of the parts of the human personage. Yet there can be found nothing else to a chariot other than the parts of it put together. Nor can there be found anything else to the human being other than the constituent parts put together. We give the name "chariot" to something made up of wheels, axles, chassis, spokes and seat when we see them organized together in one place. Even so, we give the name "human being" to the collection of parts when we see arms, legs, head and trunk organized in a certain place for a certain time. Yet Buddhists want to insist there is no self. No essence exists separate from the parts themselves. A name simply designates the bringing together of certain parts in one place. When we see parts in one place, we call it something. And that something might be "chariot" or it might be "Jim," depending upon what parts we see organized. But when the wheels fall from the chariot, when the axles are no longer there, when there is no seat remaining, then there is no chariot. The same is true of a human being, Buddhists say.

Thus, since reality is ever changing, and since no self or soul exists to anything, it is wrong to try to make something permanent of what is not permanent, to seek to possess what cannot be possessed, or even to search for a self or essence which cannot be found.

Many years ago a Tibetan monk, Milarepa, wrote a summation of this doctrinal teaching (a statement reprinted and circulated by aspiring Buddhists in America):

> All worldly pursuits have but one unavoidable and inevitable end, which is sorrow; acquisitions end in dispersion; buildings, in destruction; meetings, in separation; birth, in death. Knowing this, one should from the very first renounce acquisitions, and heaping up, building, and meeting.

A third important doctrine is the doctrine of *Dependent Origination* (paticcasamupada, Pali). This doctrine accounts for the order which prevails in the ever-changing, impermanent, essenceless world. That is, even a Buddhist is not going to deny that when we see a baby, we can know that in time this infant will grow to be an adult. The baby will not change into a frog or an elephant or a tree. Nor will it remain the same; a baby is not a baby forever.

The doctrine of Dependent Origination explains how a regular, even predictable, sequence of events occurs in the world. The doctrine states simply that every impermanent thing is caused or produced by some previous impermanent thing. All things have been produced by something else. Nothing exists independently or without a cause. All things, in turn, produce something else. Thus all things originate dependently.

There is a mutual dependence of all elements that make up reality at any particular time. All events themselves are dependent upon prior events (they would not occur without the previous events having occurred), and these dependent events give rise to new events.

Thus, all things are interdependent or mutually dependent. They have been caused by something else (thus they are dependent upon prior events) and in turn they produce something else. The adult does not appear suddenly. The adult is produced out of babyhood, child-hood and adolescence. Adulthood is dependent upon the previous causal stages in human life. Adulthood will produce another stage which might be termed "middle age," and that in turn will produce "old age." But "old age" cannot occur as an independent event. It is dependent upon the whole sequence. Thus all stages of life, all events in life, are dependent. They originate dependently. They are con-nected by a causal relation in which one stage is produced out of another stage.

The doctrine of Dependent Origination has been called the central doctrine of Buddhist thought. It is central because it guarantees that freedom from the human situation is possible. Because the doctrine purports to explain the causal relations between events, it provides hope. Faith, for a Buddhist, is belief in this doctrine—the teaching that freedom can be realized.

The secret of the doctrine is contained in the simple insight given in the "Four Noble Truths" sermon. If a person can isolate a causal relation between events, and if a cause can be eliminated, its effect is eliminated also. If an acorn is the cause of an oak tree, and if you eliminate the acorn, you also prevent the oak tree from appearing. If things and events in the world originate *dependently,* then it might be possible to do something about the occurrence or non-occurrence of some events. One needs to discover the dependence relation in any sequence of events, isolate the cause of the series, and eliminate it. Then the whole sequence of events cannot take place. If the oak tree is dependent upon the acorn, to destroy the acorn is to do away with the oak tree before it ever occurs. If old age, disease, and death are dependent upon something, to eliminate that something eliminates old age, disease, and death as well!

The doctrine of Dependent Origination is the doctrine of hope. It lays out in rather mundane terms the sequence of events that de-termine a human life:

> Craving arises from sensation, sensation from contact, contact from the six senses, the six senses from physical form, physical form from consciousness, consciousness from psychic constructions, and the psychic constructions from ignorance. . . . To repeat: Ignorance is the cause of the psychic constructions, hence is caused conscious-

ness, hence physical form, hence the six senses, hence contact, hence sensations, hence craving, hence attachment, hence becoming, hence birth, hence old age and death with all the distraction of grief and lamentation, sorrow and despair. This is the arising of the whole body of ill. . . . So we are agreed that by the complete cessation of ignorance the whole body of ill ceases.[2]

This selection from the Buddhist scripture states the dependent relations. It also identifies the fatal causal source as ignorance. Thus, wisdom will eliminate ignorance, and the eliminating of ignorance breaks the following dependent sequence of old age, disease, and death. The promised result is release.

For the Buddhist, release, or salvation, is called "Nibbana" ("Nirvana" in Sanskrit). It is best thought of as absolute peace. Instead of change, disappointment, disintegration, and death, Nirvana is quietude, peace, a permanent state. Etymologically Nirvana or Nibbana means to "blow out," to "extinguish," to "bring to an end." Thus, some have put a negative connotation upon the word, suggesting that Buddhists desire annihilation. But Buddhists look upon Nirvana as release, an opening, an entrance into what is uninhibited by the ordinary conditions of human life. To experience Nirvana is to be released from old age, disease, and death. But the experience is utterly different from the ordinary experiences common to mind, consciousness, thoughts, feelings, memories, predispositions. Nirvana is the experience of release into a dimension where such things no longer exist. What realm or dimension of reality this might be is never stated. When someone asks, the answer given is always oblique and confusing: "What is the wind like?" the questioner may be asked in return. The only answer, of course, is that the wind is something we experience, but we don't have categories of language available to describe it clearly. Even so, a Buddhist wants to insist, Nirvana is the complete absence of everything we might use to describe normal human life.

Buddhist religion begins with a pessimistic assessment of human life. But it does not counsel despair. Instead, it attempts to construct a path which will enable the person who is intensely concerned about his personal predicament to gain release. That path has nothing to do with talk about God, with prayer, with devotion, or with ceremony. The message is to the individual as though he were alone in the universe. He must act to free himself.

---

[2]Buddhist scripture, *Majjhima Nikāya* section

RECOMMENDED READING

Buddhism: A Modern Perspective. Edited by Charles S. Prebish. Pennsylvania State University Press, 1975.

Kalupahana, David J. *Buddhist Philosophy.* University Press of Hawaii, 1976.

Pardue, Peter A. *Buddhism: A Historical Introduction to Buddhist Values and the Social Forms They Have Assumed in Asia.* Macmillan, 1971.

Chapter 9

THE FAILURE OF BUDDHA'S FORMULA FOR RELEASE

Buddha met with immediate and vigorous success. Thousands chose to abandon their lifestyle to join his monastic order when they heard his message. Others hesitated to face the radical requirements of abandoning family, friends, and vocation. Nevertheless, they supported the teaching by contributing money to the growing Sangha and by feeding the monks. Monuments quickly appeared all over India, dedicated to the memory of Buddhist saints (*arhants*), and dwellings, too, for monks to inhabit during the rainy season. Many of these structures still remain in India and the countries of East and Southeast Asia to testify to the success of Buddha's teaching.

In the years following Buddha's death, many devout monks began to see problems in Buddha's teachings. In summary, three problems troubled the monks. All three are problems of a logical sort, though the logic of them was not immediately apparent.

The first problem had to do with the apparent contradiction between the wickedness of private desire for fulfillment as opposed to Buddha's insistence that people desire and seek personal enlightenment. It became apparent to some monks that a logical and moral contradiction lies at the heart of Buddha's teaching. According to the teaching, a person should want to get saved from selfishness because it is selfishness which causes human misery. The radical action of abandoning family, home, friends, and vocation to devote life to meditation promises release from selfishness.

The moral contradiction is precisely this: A person should want to get saved from desire or selfishness. But wanting to save oneself is just as selfish as any other act for selfish ends. If a person wants enlightenment, he still *wants*. And *wanting, desiring,* is the very fault which prevents enlightenment.

Any selfishly motivated act, it appears, cannot bring about selflessness. Yet a person is to be so concerned about his own salvation that he will abandon all to pursue it. Encased in the scriptural teaching and preaching about selfishness causing the human predicament are enticements toward the advantages of selfishly seeking enlightenment.

Thus Buddhism is caught in a double bind. A person must want to be saved from selfishness to achieve enlightenment. But the wanting to get saved is itself selfish. It is wanting something for oneself. This concern for personal salvation is the fundamental problem which prevents salvation.

Some Buddhists respond to this dilemma by suggesting that it is possible to want something unselfishly. That is, a person might want to get saved in order to help other people (not simply for himself). But to say this is to transform Buddha's message into something new and different. Buddha had called people to renounce the world and enter the monastic life as a means to gain personal salvation. Now many teach that a person should do it all for the sake of others. The ideal monk now is someone devoted to helping *others* gain enlightenment.

This rather creative attempt to resolve the problem of selfishness lying at the heart of Buddha's teaching is symbolized in any person called a *bodhisattva.* The earlier teaching had insisted that the ideal human is an *arhant,* a "streamwinner"—one who as an individual conquers the river of ordinary human existence and realizes the transformation of Nirvana. A *bodhisattva* is someone quite different. A *bodhisattva* abandons all, adopts the monastic life, cultivates selflessness, and eventually reaches a point of enlightenment. But just when he could enter Nirvana, he turns back, choosing to return to the life of the world in order to point the lost and despairing toward enlightenment.

A famous story illustrates the new ideal. Seven men are lost crossing a desert. They wander hopelessly and eventually are near death. Suddenly, one of them sees ahead the walls of a city. He staggers eagerly ahead, manages to climb a wall, and looks over to see a luxurious garden with a stream flowing through an orchard of fruit trees. He immediately drops over the wall and rushes to the stream of water. One after another, his companions follow him over the wall and into the orchard. But the last man looks over the wall at the water and the fruitbearing trees, then looks back at the desert. He worries that there might be others out there needing help. So he turns back to the desert and searches for other people in need of assistance.

The *bodhisattva* is someone who seeks only to help others. Thus the ideal person now spoken of by Buddhist teachers is not someone intent upon personal enlightenment, but an individual intent upon helping others. Revising earlier teaching in this way corrects the moral inconsistency. But a paradox remains: if we agree that to enter Nirvana is selfish, who then can enter Nirvana? Only a selfish person would enter Nirvana. But a selfish person cannot enter Nirvana (even to want to enter insures exclusion). So a new contradiction follows upon resolving the first: ordinary mortals cannot enter Nirvana because they are not *bodhisattvas* (they are not selfless). Only a *bodhisattva* can enter Nirvana; but a *bodhisattva* will not enter Nirvana because he is a *bodhisattva*.

This new explanation to bypass the moral dilemma eliminates all discussion concerning the goal of the religion. No one, it must be admitted now, can enter Nirvana. Soon a vague teaching about paradise (sukhavati) replaces talk about Nirvana. Paradise is a way station, a "happy land," where those capable of enjoying ultimate bliss wait until all creatures are ready to cross into Nirvana. In short, Buddhists begin to talk of a paradise, a pre-heaven.

Yet another problem surfaces: Why did Siddhartha Gautama, the Buddha, enter Nirvana? Do not the texts say that he experienced Nirvana? How could he act so selfishly?

Gradually discussions among the monks produced an answer. The question of Buddha's entrance into Nirvana is irrelevant because he was not mere human, he was divine. Buddha was a manifestation upon earth of the divine essence. He was not flesh and blood. He just appeared as though he were human. He was an illusion, an apparition. People thought they saw and heard a human being; but they did not. Siddhartha Gautama was God showing himself to the world in order to preach enlightenment.

Buddhist teaching began to advocate an incarnation doctrine. God entered the world, they said. But it is a peculiar twist on an incarnation theme: God did not actually take on human flesh. Rather, God projected himself as though He were a human. Siddhartha was a mirage, a phantasm, an illusion. But since he was not human, he could enter Nirvana. Siddhartha was seen to die, but his death was but God abandoning the illusory body and returning to His divine essence.

With such a resolution to the question of Siddhartha's entrance to Nirvana, Buddhism made a second great adjustment to the early teaching. The adjustment was forced by the logic of the early teaching itself. But it forces Buddhists to accept a good deal of extra baggage. If Buddha was God showing himself to the world, then realization might be achieved without abandoning the world, without becoming a monk. Maybe one might simply pray to Buddha. Maybe there are rituals or ceremonies which might be pleasing to Buddha. Maybe Buddha's favor might be won by good deeds. And in fact, a whole series of rituals, prayers, and ceremonies are popular among some Buddhists.

Developing the doctrine that Buddha was God revealing himself to human beings resolved a problem. It also changed Buddhism into a theistic religion employing prayers, ceremonies, thank offerings, and other means to win salvation. The new Buddhism is quite different from the austere Buddhism encouraged initially.

Yet a third problem—this one with revolutionary consequences—lay in the area of doctrinal consistency. The doctrines of Imperman-ence, No Self, and Dependent Origination contradict one another.

These doctrines as initially stated and as practiced were useful devices to assist meditation. A monk is encouraged by these teachings to meditate on the process of change, contemplating the occurrence of an idea in the mind, its duration, and its disappearance. Meditation consisted of noting the rise of a mental event (a thought), its duration, and its vanishing, only to be followed by the rise of another mental event, its duration, and its passing. A monk was encouraged to note that each event is tied to a preceding event and to a subsequent event by a dependent relation. One thought gives rise to another, and on and on. In the quiet contemplation of the sequence of mental events, a sense of impermanence results. The lesson becomes clear: All is impermanent, all things are but parts of an ongoing sequence of events. Attachment to any event, any thought, any thing should be avoided.

Yet, however valuable these teachings might be as devices to assist meditation, eventually a person must ask, do they provide a consistent and credible description of reality? Are the assertions concerning impermanence true? Does *everything* change? Is there no permanent essence to anything? Is there really no self? Does the process of change occur by dependent origination?

One procedure we can follow in analyzing is to consider the con-sequences of holding to a doctrine. If a person holds to the doctrine of Impermanence, a common-sense understanding of the world is no longer possible. If Impermanence as a doctrine is the case, then a person must ask, What constitutes the past, present, and future of any event? Clearly, the past of an event is not something to be con-sidered as real, since each event is impermanent. The memory of "pastness" is something to be obliterated from the mind, since memory is a form of grasping or attachment.

Moreover, the doctrine implies that the future is not to be considered as something real either. Nor should it even be anticipated. Anticipating the future is a form of grasping. All that exists is the instantaneous present, a moment now here, but now gone.

The immediate occurrence of events as momentary happenings constitutes reality as described by the Buddhist doctrine of Impermanence. The past does not exist; the future is without existence also. There is only the *instantaneous* present, the immediate moment. That alone is real.

Difficulties with this sort of thinking should be clear. It destroys common-sense thinking and acting. All of us act daily on the assumption that the immediate past is as real as the present and that the future is something for which we had better prepare ourselves. Getting out of bed in the morning, shopping, going to work, cooking a meal, nurturing and helping a child to grow—all of these human activities are based on the assumption that the past is real and the future is something which will soon occur. Ordinary thinking demands that we deal seriously with a real past and anticipate a real future.

But the spiritual implications of the teachings are even more problematic. What happens to the Karma doctrine if the Impermanence doctrine is held? How can an event's effect follow at some later time if every event is impermanent? Does not the Karma doctrine say that past acts *determine* future conditions? Does this not imply that something permanent behind the veil of impermanent events forces some consequence at a later time? Does the doctrine of Impermanence contradict the doctrine of Karma?

Moreover, how can Nirvana be won? The assumption behind the teaching about release is that some human act or acts will bring about the realization of Nirvana—that is, some acts will cause Nirvana to be an experience. But how can a series of instantaneous, impermanent acts make or generate a permanent state of bliss, Nirvana?

We find similar difficulties when we study the consequences of holding to the doctrines of No Self and Dependent Origination. How can Nirvana be a real experience if there is no self to experience it? How can there be such a thing as an "experience" without an "experiencer"? How can rebirth occur without a self to be reborn? Why do we have memory of the past when the doctrine of No Self maintains that there is no self surviving from moment to moment? Or, what is the dependence relation that makes events happen in an orderly, sequential way? Why is it that events are coordinated in a regular, predictable sequence? Why is it that when an acorn is planted, it is always an oak tree that grows from it and not a cherry tree or an elephant? Does a dependency relation sufficiently explain all that occurs in a causal relation? Does that explain causal relations? If not, must a person doubt Buddha's promise that eliminating the cause of bondage will bring release? If the cause-effect relation between misery and its cause cannot be precisely defined, what confidence can be put in the teaching?

Any rationalist examining Buddhism will confront a suspicion that Buddhists have made an inaccurate description of the predicament. And if the description of the predicament is wrong, salvation cannot be assured.

Buddhism breaks on these three areas of intellectual difficulty. Questions concerning the moral propriety of becoming a monk, the nature of the Buddha, and the logical consistency of his major doctrines force Buddhists to either reconstruct Buddhist thought or to choose a dogmatic assertion of the literal teaching. Some Buddhists choose to hold to a dogmatic stance. These maintain that Buddha said what he said; the scriptures record it; and the appropriate response is for people to practice austerity, to meditate, and to reach a condition of nonattachment. They consider speculative questions useless, a waste of time and effort. The poison of human existence spreads its misery. One must hear the word and respond appropriately.

Other Buddhists argue that there is an explanation for these apparent contradictions. Buddha was not so foolish and ignorant as to speak things which prove to be nonsense. These Buddhists presented a new explanation of the Buddha word.

The conservative, dogmatic Buddhists hold to the "teaching of the elders." They maintain that the original doctrines are sufficient to bring release. They appeal to the analogy of a raft. When a person crosses a river with a raft, he does not pick it up on the far side and carry it along on his journey. The raft is good for crossing the river; but it is useless equipment once we reach the far bank. In like manner, doctrines are useful means toward achieving release. But once a person has fully used them, they need not be carried along. A doctrine's value is in what it *does* for a person in his situation. Teachings of the Buddha, these people maintain, are useful devices for attaining release. Once release is attained, there is no point considering them further.

Conservative Buddhists align themselves with the traditional teaching, and they take the name of *theravada* to show that they affirm the historic message. The strongholds of conservative Buddhism today are South and Southeast Asia, the countries of Sri Lanka, Burma,

Thailand, Cambodia, and Vietnam. A lively religious establishment centered on the community of monks (the sangha) continues by espousing asceticism and individual enlightenment as an ideal to pursue.

A "NEW EXPLANATION" OF BUDDHA'S TEACHING

Many Buddhists have chosen a new explanation of what Buddha meant when he preached. The essentials of the explanation are ancient. They probably date from the second century B.C. in a group of texts called *Prajnaparamita Sutras,* "Aphorisms of the Greater Wisdom." But it was not until the second century A.D. that anyone formulated a specific view. His name was Nagarjuna, and he was a major thinker of India.

The "new explanation" of Buddha's teaching hinges on what has been called the "silence" of Buddha. In the texts which record Buddha's teaching, Buddha meets certain questions with silence. He refused to answer, the texts assert. The questions became known as "the inexpressibles," or "the questions which tend not toward edification." Buddha must have believed that some questions were not worth asking because any answer which might be given would not make any difference concerning the human condition of old age, disease, and death.

The "new explanation" maintains that in this silence lies the secret teaching Buddha was attempting to convey. The silence was a sophisticated illustration of Buddha's main point, it is held. That point is that reality cannot be stated in doctrines, assertions, categories, propositions. Reality transcends human thought, names, concepts and ideas. Reality cannot be grasped by the mind; it cannot be contained by words.

The new teaching is that Buddha was silent because he knew and wanted his hearers to understand that any answer given to certain questions would force his hearers to fall back upon either dogmatism or into logical contradictions. Buddha was maintaining, so the new explanation goes, that reality is completely, totally, utterly indescribable.

These Buddhists insist that Buddha was telling people that there are no answers, there are no explanations. Buddha did not intend to state a system of doctrines and ideas and explanations about life and death. Instead, he was offering a criticism of all assertions people might have made which allege to be answers to questions about the human situation. This, they say, is the real "middle way" which Buddha was teaching. It is the middle way which cuts directly through all disputes about religion, philosophy, and science by saying that there are no final answers, no solutions, there is no escape, no salvation. There is only "emptiness."

Nagarjuna, the major proponent of the "new explanation," presented a sustained argument to show that every conventional explanation about the nature of reality was absurd. His essays are curious documents because he never tried to replace what he criticizes with something new or different. Instead, he reduces any attempt to explain life to logical absurdity. He criticizes rebirth, the doctrine of Karma, the contemporary notions of space, time, causality, motion, rest, Nirvana, and even the notion that there might be someone such as a Buddha. All ideas, all beliefs are destroyed by Nagarjuna. All ideas are absurd, he maintains. There is nothing to cling to, nothing to believe, no hope, no salvation. There is only emptiness, he said.

Nagarjuna's arguments attempt to show that the human mind is incapable of grasping reality. He denies any view of causation, a central teaching in the quest for liberation. He notes four prevailing explanations concerning the causal process: (1) The effects of a cause must lie within the cause. (2) The effect of a cause is completely different from the cause. (3) The cause and its effect are both the same and different from one another. (4) There really is no such thing as a cause-effect relationship.

Nagarjuna examined all four of the possible explanations and found each one unsatisfactory. If an effect is contained in a cause, he insisted there is really no significant difference between a cause and its effect. They are actually the same. But that denies what we see happening all the time, for oak trees do not actually reside in acorns, yet acorns cause oak trees.

Some insist that a cause and its effect are two distinct happenings; the effect is not contained in the cause. Then there is no logical reason to expect an oak tree to follow from the planting of an acorn, since anything might emerge. If we state that a cause and its effect are the same as one another, yet different too, we are giving a logically absurd view. We cannot say that the effect is both contained in the cause and not contained in the cause. Finally, if we attempt to argue that there is no such thing as cause-effect relations, then our argument denies what we ourselves assert, because any argument causes its conclusions.

In this way Nagarjuna dispatches to the scrap heap as many views as he can find of time, space, motion, Nirvana, and Buddha. No assertion about reality escapes his critical eye. He will not even believe any talk about a Buddha. He leaves his readers with nothing but emptiness, *s'unyata*. Reality is only an interdependent grouping of events with no event standing alone. Therefore, there are no in-dependent answers, no explanations. All things are interdependent. There can be no solution, no explanation, to the problem of human life with its process of birth, disease, old age, and death.

In short, the "new explanation" asserts that there is only empti-ness, there is only a void. Buddha was teaching that Nirvana is sam-sara (release is the same as the round of birth and death) and samsara is Nirvana (the round of birth and death is the same as release). That is all there is. There is nowhere to go, nothing to do, no one to pray to, nothing to hope for, nothing to work toward, no heaven, no hell. There is only emptiness!

For many, such a message dashes all hope. But for Nagarjuna and his followers, this constituted the central message of Buddha. The central message of this Buddhism is frightening, even terrifying to someone looking for a message of hope in times of despair. It demands a radical change of mind, of attitude, of thought. It demands what they call enlightenment. Such insight is true freedom, Buddhists main-tain. It is a freedom from beliefs, hopes, fears, dogmas, terrors. There are no explanations. There is only emptiness!

THE IDEA OF EMPTINESS APPLIED TO LIFE

The new explanation of Buddha's teaching persuaded many Bud-dhists to reject the older views and doctrines. Some, of course, con-tinued to hold to the old doctrines. But many abandoned Buddha's literal words in favor of more liberal views. If, in fact, the old teaching could not be taken literally, then anything which might help a person to realize peace in life might be legitimate. No idea, no ritual, no symbol, no doctrine can be looked upon as having any significant authority. A person is free to do what he will. Reality is empty. Nirvana is samsara, and samsara is Nirvana.

The new explanation quickly spread east to Tibet, China, Korea, and Japan. Later it spread the other direction also and influenced some Western thinkers. A major school of Eastern thought which had a significant impact upon Western thought is Zen Buddhism of Japan. Though the origins of Zen can be traced back through China to India, the Japanese style of Zen meditation and teaching dominates European and American notions of Buddhism.

Zen influenced many Americans in the late 1940s, 1950s, and 1960s. The so-called "Beat generation" of poets and writers of the 1950s and 1960s borrowed heavily from Zen notions of language and

religion. The writings of American Zen spokesmen such as Jack Ker-
ouack and Alan Watts attracted cult followings in many sections of
the United States.

Zen attracts many because it never pushes a creedal formula or
doctrinal statement. Rather, it advocates a particular style of living,
a style critical of conventional society's mores. Zen aims to free the
mind and emotions from an attachment to "mere things" and material
comforts so that a new style of living might be realized. And Zen
itself provides a technique for the realization of emptiness. Such a
realization reveals that other people are living in emotional and spiritual poverty. At the same time, it gives a sense of personal freedom
and liberation.

According to Zen teaching, experiencing the reality of the emptiness of all things is to realize something which cannot be communicated in words. In fact, most human beings are in bondage because
they have been brainwashed into thinking that conventional ways to
speak and write are good and true.

Zen claims to free people from conventional words, ideas, values
and categories by breaking the hold of these things upon the human
mind. They hold men captive.

The tyranny of words, Zen advocates maintain, is clear from a
look at what words do to people. They are treacherous, for they create
a false world for people, a substitute world, a world that dilutes the
intensity of direct experience. Words stand in the way of direct experience.

Words may make the world manageable for people. When confronted with sickness, disease, death, people look to words to help
soften the blows of these things. Words bring comfort. When confronted with bewildering or inexplicable situations, words somehow
clarify things for people.

However, the manageable world created by words also dilutes
reality, Zen advocates maintain. Words detract from or obstruct the
truth. They make reality innocuous, even fraudulent because they
shelter people from reality.

But the most significant fact about words, say Zen Buddhists, is
that words create a trap. The trap has two aspects to it: (1) People
are bewitched into thinking that words provide a correct picture of
things. Politicians, advertisers, and charlatans of all types use this
trap regularly. (2) People are trapped into thinking that they can fill
their inner vacuum, their sense of lostness and aloneness, with words.
So they rush from one set of doctrines, one set of words, to another.
Yet all they ever find is another set of words piled upon words.

This critique of modern culture and religion exposes several real problems. Indeed, evidence abounds regarding the treachery of words as Zen Buddhists describe it. Zen holds an appeal because it is a technique for breaking the hold of words upon people.

The technique requires meditation under the guidance of a teacher. The peculiar meditation and teaching process are both designed to break the hold of words. And breaking the hold of words means to literally shatter them.

But how can words be shattered? The teacher finds what beliefs, doctrines, or values bind a person. Then the teacher provides a student with what is called *koan,* a riddle or puzzle. The student retires to a meditation hall to consider the problem contained in the puzzle.

The *koan* puzzle is a puzzle like no other. It states, usually as a question, some formulation of words which appear contradictory or even absurd. "You have heard the sound of two hands clapping. What is the sound of one hand clapping?" Or "What was the appearance of your face before your ancestors were born?"

At first a student might wish to dismiss these puzzles as nonsense. But the teacher forces the student to face the puzzle with the intense pressure which the human mind can bring to bear upon something over a period of hours, days, and even months of meditating. At some point, the mind cracks. The words, the categories, that once forced the mind to consider the puzzle in a logical way suddenly fall away, they break. The mind leaps to a new dimension, what is thought to be a new insight into the nature of reality. Words are transcended; the mind confronts reality as it is, unobstructed by words.

Another way to consider what happens in Zen meditation is to picture an individual human being standing just outside the world. As he grows and matures, a screen or grid of ideas, values, attitudes, and categories gradually grows between the individual and the outside world. The grid is a part of the mind, yet it is a filter through which the individual perceives and experiences the world. For example, as a child grows to adulthood, his parents, his friends, his school, his church all give him a vocabulary as a way to understand the world he experiences. Certain attitudes and values accompany the words, so that the child is trained in proper conduct. He is told what is "good." He is told what is "bad." Eventually society constructs a grid screen through which he sees everything.

This grid built by childhood training—a grid composed of words, categories, attitudes, and moral values—stands between a person and the real world. And people use the grid as a way to relate to the world. They use it as a way to understand themselves as well.

But the grid is culturally determined, say Zen Buddhists. The grid is artificial and relative. Society forces it upon people. It does not and cannot correspond to reality.

The grid and dependence upon the grid constitute bondage, Zen teaches. The grid must be shattered so that the individual can confront true reality rather than the reality filtered through the categories of the grid. A shattering of the grid will bring direct insight, enlightenment, realization. Zen is a technique for shattering the grid.

The experience of having the grid shattered cannot be communicated in words. The experience is one that is beyond words. Some claim that former prejudices, hatreds, and resentments are shattered along with the words that had formerly sustained them. And others insist that Zen discipline brought them to the edge of lunacy, but then freed them from the threat of schizophrenia and psychosis.

THE FAILURE OF ZEN

The earlier doctrines of Buddhism failed for many people because they could not provide a rational, coherent, consistent description of the human predicament and its solution. Zen Buddhism and the "new explanation" fail because they build upon an inadequate and fictitious foundation.

This false foundation rests upon Zen's presupposition that language is a purely arbitrary set of symbols, unrelated to reality. Zen builds its therapy techniques on the assumption that a chasm exists between words and what they point to. Language does not and cannot mirror the actual structure of the world, Zen holds. Language is artificial, relative, and unrelated to things as they actually are.

Zen goes on to maintain that the rules of language are also arbitrary, relative, and subject to alteration. No word, no sentence, no category or statement actually states what is the case in the real world. Words are mere symbols constructed by humans and arranged in certain ways to conform to a particular grammar. Neither words nor the grammatical structure of any human language can correspond to reality, say Buddhists.

Buddhists conclude that language stands in the way of seeing things as they are. They maintain that a veil stands between the human mind and reality. Thus, language and its hold upon people must be shattered, broken. Only then will a person be free to see things as they are. In fact, say Buddhists, language binds people, it stunts them, it traps them, and it holds them.

But this view of language and its relation to reality is false. Language evolves from the human mind's encounter with reality. Language's logical structures correspond to the structure of reality. Rules for the use of language are not at all arbitrary or subject to alteration. Language and its rules are structured by the nature of reality, and are universal. One ignores the rules at the cost of speaking or writing unintelligibly.

The principle of Noncontradiction illustrates the point that language does correspond to reality. The principle maintains that something cannot be said to exist and to not exist at the same time. A thing may exist or it may not exist. But it cannot both exist and not exist at once.

The principle of Noncontradiction states a necessity which is built into both language and into reality. The principle forces intelligible sentences to mirror reality. It forces the conclusion that it is impossible to make sense by saying that something both exists and does not exist at once. But the principle shows that contradiction is not simply semantic nonsense. It is nonsense concerning what is really the case.

Some thinkers have attempted to skirt this issue by asserting that the principle of Noncontradiction holds only to language but not to reality. They argue that only our particular way of using language prevents us from seeing that something can both exist and not exist at once, or that the same surface might be both green and red at the same time, or that a chair can both be in a room and not in a room at the same time. Some would even go so far as to insist that the principle of Noncontradiction holds only to some languages and not to others. They suggest that without our present grammar of the English language, we could accurately describe reality by saying that I am both at my desk working and not at my desk working.

Such views are obviously nonsense! Language conforms to the structure of things at a very basic level. No matter how imprecise it may sometimes be, no matter how it may be abused by some people, and regardless of how liars and cheats abuse it, language does ultimately conform to the structure of reality. The principle of Noncontradiction should make that clear to anyone who cares to think about it.

Building a religious system on a contrary view is both foolish and subversive. It is foolish because it implies that reality has no structure which can be known and communicated by words or symbols. But modern physical science constantly implies the opposite: Scientific discoveries often are discoveries dealing with the structure of things.

The Buddhist view is subversive because it encourages people to discard reason in the contemplation of life and the world. Experiences which bypass reason to probe what is ultimately real must be considered with some suspicion. Experiences as well as statements must conform to the order built into the nature of things or they are simply nonsensical gibberish. One escapes the so-called bondage of logic and language only at the cost of a more ominous bondage in a wilderness of nonsense.

RECOMMENDED READING

Blanshard, Brand. *Reason and Analysis.* Open Court, 1964.
Danto, Arthur. *Mysticism and Morality.* Basic Books, 1972.
Understanding the New Religions. Edited by Jacob Needleman and George Baker. Seabury Press, 1978.

Chapter 10

ISLAM—RULE-KEEPING AS RELIGION

Islam is the youngest of the world's major religions. It claims, however, to be the oldest, holding that it follows the truths established by God since the beginning. It is generally not categorized as an "Asian" religion because it emerged out of the Middle East, the birth-place of Jewish and Christian faiths. But its 800 million adherents today live mainly in Asia. Christianity and Judaism moved west; Islam moved east.

Associated with the religion of Islam is the name of the prophet Muhammad. He was a reformer, one who calls people to be consistent and live according to fundamental principles of faith. The religious culture Muhammad stepped into in seventh century Arabia was a mix of Jewish, Christian, and polytheistic nature worship. His mes-sage was a call to return to basic themes of the Jewish-Christian tradition. Yet he maintained that what he himself had said completed, fulfilled, and perfected the best that Jews and Christians had ever said. Muhammad, Muslims claim, was the last of the prophets and the one who transmitted God's Word perfectly.

FUNDAMENTAL ASSERTIONS OF ISLAMIC FAITH

The history of the Muslim faith, conquest, community life, and theology is tied directly to certain fundamental beliefs which shaped Muhammad's message and the continuing message of Muslim scrip-ture (*Koran* or *Qur'an*). The beliefs shape Muslim thought and prac-tice, but they also set the limits of such thought and practice.

A first claim of the faith is that Islam really did not begin with the prophet Muhammad. It began at the day of creation, if not before. When God created the world, He decreed that the forces of nature were to act according to His divinely ordained pattern. God established natural law; and nature acts according to it—inevitably, perfectly, even blindly. The patterned behavior of nature bears witness to the Creator, Muslims insist.

At the same time as God established a natural order, He ordained an order for humans as well. He established a right way for people to live. The rules or laws show how people should relate to God and to one another.

God created human beings different than nature. Men, unlike nature, can choose whether or not to live according to His pattern. If they live correctly, they flourish. If they break the law of God built into the natural order, they bring chaos upon themselves.

God never leaves mankind without guidance concerning His law, however. As soon as man was created, he was given the law. Adam was but the first of many prophets to whom God revealed His will. Human history opened with clear knowledge concerning the will of God and His pattern for life, but Adam proved to be disobedient. His descendants neglected, forgot, lost, or falsified the message.

After Adam, God in His mercy continued to send additional messengers. But the story is repeated: Men forget, distort, or ignore the revelation. Abraham, Moses, Jesus—all these appeared as prophets to reinstitute the law. Moses' followers put into practice important ideas, but they allowed their copies of the text to be corrupted. Soon they came to believe that the divine message applied only to themselves (they began to think of themselves as a "chosen" people). Jesus was sent to correct the errors of the Jews. His followers understood the universalism of the message (they preached the good news to non-Jews). But Christians, Muslims insist, made the mistake of worshiping the messenger. Christians committed a twofold crime, Muslims maintain. They deified the messenger, denying the oneness of God. They distorted the message so that it emphasized personal salvation and piety rather than the construction of the social and political order prescribed by God.

In one final, dramatic move God salvaged the human race by fully and effectively injecting His guidance into human affairs. Muhammad, the last of the prophets, fully delivered, interpreted, and lived the message with undeviating precision. The community of submitters (Muslims) that he established has been given the task to faithfully preserve the message and to carry it to the ends of the earth. This time there was no error, no distortion, no neglect of the message.

Muslims maintain that those who submit (Islam) reconstruct a community in accordance with eternal truth. The Islamic community embodies the eternal pattern for human life in the world. At first the group consisted of the inhabitants of only two Arabian cities, Medina and Mecca. But the community grew to a point where men from almost every country, race, color, and climate now are a part of the group. And all members of the community are known as submitters, acceptors, Muslims. People today may approach God only by participating in the Islamic community as it endeavors to realize the rule of God on earth.

The Muslims' fundamental message is a message of how to live in the world. It is carried by a book, but it is also being lived by a community of believers. Their success (or failure) testifies to the soundness of the message.

MUHAMMAD AND HIS TIME

Arabia in the seventh century A.D. was a sparsely populated land of nomadic peoples. Mecca, on the western coast, was a thriving commercial town at the juncture of caravan routes crossing the Arabian desert. In the heart of the city stood the Ka'bah sanctuary, a shrine celebrating the fall of a meteorite (an event referred to as early as 60 B.C. by a Roman historian).

Associated with the reverence given the Black Stone (the Ka'bah) was a sacred oasis and numerous gods and goddesses. Together with the shrine and its well were the attractions of fertility ceremonies and priestly rituals designed to hold at bay the numerous demonic spirits who robbed graves, thrived on human flesh, and disturbed and terrorized the lives of ordinary people.

One god among the many associated with the Ka'bah outranked all the others. He was known as Allah, the Creator. "Allah" is the same word in Arabic as the Hebrew "Elohim" and the Aramaic "Elah." There is reason to think that the Jews' Yahweh (Jehovah), the Christians' "God the Father who is in heaven," and "Allah" referred somewhere and at some time to the same God.

As a trading center, Mecca contained all of the religious-political-commercial clamor and corruption which trading centers are prone to encourage. Religious hucksterism was scarcely distinguishable from institutionally established practices. In fact, accounts of life in Mecca prior to Muhammad suggest the worst, most degenerate forms of vice mixed with religion imaginable.

Muhammad was born sometime around the year A.D. 570. Apparently he was orphaned while young and brought up under the care of a grandfather and an uncle. Both men were members of the Arabic tribe responsible for ritual activities associated with the Ka'bah and the holy well of Zamzam. As a young man Muhammad journeyed to Syria, and there he might have learned something of Nestorian Christianity (officially condemned as heretical, but thriving in Syria at the time).

Muhammad married a woman named Khadija, some fifteen years older than he and very wealthy. All of their sons died young, but a daughter named Fatima survived.

There settled upon Muhammad in mid-life a conviction that a final judgment by God was imminent. If a judgment were to occur, he wondered why God did not send a prophet to the Arab people. Under a settled conviction of judgment, Muhammad structured his life in such a way as to spend long periods of time in secluded prayer. One night, referred to by Muslims as "The Night of Power and Excellence," the angel Gabriel appeared and commanded him to speak.

> Recite in the name of the Lord who created,
> Created man of a blood-clot.
> Recite: And thy Lord is the most generous,
> Who taught by the pen,
> Taught man what he knew not. . . .[1]

Muhammad had some initial doubts about the authenticity of his vision and the message he received. But soon he settled in his mind that he was a prophet of Allah, the one God. And then new revelations came to him.

But trouble followed his claims to speak for Allah. His messages threatened those who lived by preaching and practicing the popular religions. Muhammad's messages denounced the worship of images and the fertility festivities. Persecution accompanied resistance. But his wife, some members of his household (including Ali, the son of an uncle) and Abu Bakr, a merchant of some standing in the city, listened and converted.

The message Muhammad stated in various ways was that people were to submit to Allah, demonstrating their submission by various acts. The acts of submission, later revelations claimed, were simple but necessary signs of allegiance to Allah. One needed to confess, "There is no God but Allah and Muhammad is His prophet." One must pray five times daily (with congregational prayer at noon on Friday); give alms in the form of a tithe; fast during the lunar month of Ramadan; and view the "House of God"—the Ka'bah at Mecca.

Important events intervened between Muhammad's initial messages and the creation of a community of believers. A plot was laid

---
[1] Surah 96

to kill Muhammad. But he and his friends escaped, fleeing to the nearby city of Medina. Muhammad had been invited earlier to the city of Medina, and his escape in 622 to that city marks year one of the new order of God's rule on earth, according to Muslims. Muhammad received a warm welcome in Medina. He set about to reorder life in the city according to the principles he derived from the revelations.

Muhammad set up a religious government with himself as the prophet who knew the will of God. He built a mosque for public worship and ordered prostration in prayer to be directed toward Jerusalem. But when Jews of the city resisted his message, Muhammad determined that Muslims must prostrate themselves toward the city of Mecca.

After only eight years, Muhammad turned out an army of 10,000 men. His old city of Mecca offered but token resistance to the soldiers inspired by Muhammad's messages. When Mecca was captured, Muhammad circled the Ka'bah Stone seven times, then destroyed the images of the gods and goddesses. He rededicated the holy places of Ka'bah and the well of Zamzam. And he changed the laws and established a theocracy with himself as God's spokesman.

But then, quite suddenly, Muhammad died in 632. He had failed to name a successor. Nor had he stated a procedure for selecting a successor. The issue of succession split the community of submitters. The split remains to this day, dividing Muslims into two great branches of Islam—the Sunni branch and the Shi'ite branch.

Abu Bakr, the early convert, was seen by many to be Muhammad's natural successor. Abu Bakr lasted only a year before he too died. Real trouble began after the death of the third successor, or Caliph. The election and appointment of Ali, Muhammad's son-in-law, was contested by powerful Muslims of the Umayyad clan in Syria. Ali, realizing the threat of opposition, attempted to move his government to Iraq. But assassins put an end to him and his rule.

From the controversies over succession and the assassination of Ali came the Shia movement—a movement tying itself directly to the claims of Ali as legitimate successor. After the death of Ali, however, the Umayyad consolidated rule in Damascus, Syria. They took the name Sunna to identify their allegiance to the customs and precedents established by the prophet Muhammad. The Umayyads established a great order which was superseded only by the later Abbasid dynasty of Baghdad.

The Shi'ites, on the other hand, insisted on a rival theory of succession. Ali, they claimed, was really the first successor. Hassan succeeded Ali. The third true leader was Husain, who met a tragic death in battle with his rivals. The death of Husain is mourned annually by Shi'ite Muslims. The great split, then, was not a matter of doctrine or theological differences, but of who should wield power on earth. Shi'ites claim that successorship to Muhammad is essentially a spiritual office—an office of prayer leader, an *imam*. Such leadership is transmitted not by election or even deliberation among powerful people, but by an anointing of God. The word *imam* literally means "leader." Shi'ites eventually formulated the belief that a divine spark is transferred from one *imam* to another. Muhammad was an *imam* carrying the divine spark, and he passed it to Ali, Shi'ites claim.

Disagreements exist among Shi'ites as to how many *imams* there have been in the world. A majority hold that there have been twelve, the last one living in the tenth century. He is thought of as being in "hiding," since he disappeared without a trace; but he will return as a *mahdi*, a "divinely guided one," it is said, in the end times to redirect the world toward righteousness and peace.

Today Shi'ite Islam is strong in Iraq and Iran. Iran has recently established Shi'ite faith as the norm for government and social life. The Ayatollah ("sign of Allah") Khomeini of Iran headed the movement to overthrow the imperial rule of the Shah. He falls into a line of spiritual leadership which believes itself to be ordained by Allah to reform the world by establishing a divine form of government in the world.

THE KORAN AS REVELATION

Muhammad's message came to him as a series of revelations. He presented them to his followers in piecemeal fashion throughout his career until the time of his death. After his death the messages were collected into a book called Koran (or Qurán). This book serves as the fundamental authority for the faith of all Muslims.

Muhammad and his followers claimed that the Koran derives from a heavenly original, a book that is with God. The heavenly original has been partially revealed to men from time to time through Jewish and Christian prophets. It is God's practice, the prophet maintained, to use books as the normal mode of revelation.

Most people familiar with the history of literature and the techniques of making books are surprised by Muhammad's willingness to give divine endorsement to what was at that time an elite form of communication among the nomadic people of the Arabian deserts. What mode of communication might strike Muhammad as divine

today (given the options among computers, lasers, and video equipment) is uncertain. Comtemporary Muslims avoid discussing the issue, so there is no official explanation concerning why God would
wish to limit himself to a communications technology of a specific
time and place. Moreover, the question of why God would choose
Arabic as the language of revelation pleads for an answer too.

The facts insist that Muhammad held that God communicates
best by the written page. From the beginning with Adam it has been
done, Muhammad maintained. And from the beginning men have
distorted and corrupted the eternal message. Only Muhammad's
statements contained in the Koran, which he recited under the guidance of the angel Gabriel, are the true, complete, and final revelation
of God to mankind.

Muslim theologians three centuries after Muhammad's death un-
derlined the significance of Muhammad's recitations in their eyes by
asserting that the Koran is uncreated and co-eternal with God. A
story detailing the call of Muhammad often accompanies any claim
concerning the miraculous nature of the revelation. When Muhammad was keeping his lonely vigil in a cave near Mecca, the story says,
the angel Gabriel forced him to speak. Muhammad resisted. But the
angel seized him by the throat, choked him, and threatened his life
until Muhammad agreed to speak.

The story is used to point out that there was no initiative on the
part of Muhammad to be a prophet. Revelation came to him against
his will and in spite of his resistance to it. Muhammad's sole task, it
is said, was to repeat what was spoken to him by the angel. He could
claim no special qualities or knowledge for himself, nor could he assign
any significance to his own character or personality. Allah simply
chose Muhammad, and the angel made him deliver the revelation.
Moreover, Muhammad himself was illiterate, Muslims often claim,
and incapable of composing a book of such elevated style as the Arabic
Koran.

The story of the Koran being revealed to Muhammad gives rise
to some interesting aspects of Muslim faith. First, the Koran is considered to be the foremost authority in all matters—spiritual and legal.
It lays down the proper way for people to live. A pious Muslim finds
it inconceivable that any other source of authority or information
about life might be placed alongside or above the Koran. Also, the
Koran determines the typical Muslim method of problem solving. The
method is essentially deductive. A person faced with any problem
need merely consult the revelation and extract from it the principles
for solving the problem. Any situation to be found in life is dealt

with—at least in principle—by the divine revelation of the Koran, Muslims believe.

Such a view of the Koran is crucial to the development of Muslim theology (or, one might say, to the failure of Muslims to develop a theology independent of the literal statements of the Koran). Christians and Jews regard their scriptures as revelation, to be sure. But Jewish and Christian reverence for their books is not officially defined or endorsed in the way Muslim reverence is. Jews and Christians do not hold to a *dictation* view of revelation. But Muslims maintain that God through the angel *dictated* the text of the Koran.

We can only guess at the exact state of the materials of the Koran when Muhammad died. Part of the text may have been committed to writing under Muhammad's supervision. The Koran as it stands today was collected and put together under the third Caliph, Uthman (644-656). He wished to avoid conflicts among the faithful about various versions of the book which existed at the time. Uthman ordered an official text prepared, based upon a document in the possession of the daughter of the second Caliph. Other versions of the Koran in circulation were replaced by the Uthmanic version.

A first encounter with the Koran is puzzling because the official collators paid scant attention to the chronology or to the logical connections between subjects. The messages range from vivid warnings concerning the punishment of sinners to stories of former prophets to expositions of detailed rules for living. And then there are the mystical passages which seem to bear little relation to the detailed expositions or dire warnings of earlier sections.

It is helpful to keep in mind that the text to Muslims is no mere compilation. They view it as a record of inspired utterances delivered over a long period of time, each one couched in a style of speaking and writing appropriate to a specific occasion. And the text itself is called a "Recitation" (Koran). For Muslims, it is not a historical document. Instead, it is an immediate and unconditioned revelation of God's will for mankind expressed in His own eternal words.

For Muslim faithful, no translation accurately transmits the message of the Koran. The Arabic edition is the true Koran, and even that is but a copy of the original laid up in heaven.

Such a view of the Koran is one which later Muslims needed to explain more fully and with greater precision when confronted with claims to revelation from Jews, Christians, Buddhists, Zoroastrians, and Hindus. It is one thing to hold to a dictation theory of revelation—as Muslims do. It is another to make the text speak in some literal fashion to men across cultural boundaries and through time.

Chapter 11

ISLAM'S EXPANSION

The early years of the new Islamic community were a dramatic success. Muslim armies marched with triumph everywhere. When the prophet Muhammad died in 632, ten years after his migration (*hijra*) from Mecca to Medina, the new religion controlled the whole of the Arabian Peninsula. The population may have been sparse, but the geographic area under Muslim control was vast.

Muslim armies rapidly overran the nations of the Fertile Crescent, from Syria to the Persian Gulf, and then moved to conquer Egypt. Twenty-five years after Muhammad's death, the religion had reached east as far as Afghanistan and went into Tunisia, North Africa. By the early eighth century, the religion had reached Morocco and was moving through Spain into France. Islam was on its way to conquering Europe when Charles Martel defeated the Muslim Moors at Tours, France, in A.D. 732. At the same time it moved deep into Asia, north and east into what is now Pakistan. Conquered territories included the contemporary nations of Spain, Portugal, Morocco, Algeria, Tunisia, Libya, Egypt, South Yemen, Yemen, Saudi Arabia, Oman and the Emirates, Kuwait, Israel, Jordan, Syria, Lebanon, Iraq, Georgia of the U.S.S.R., Iraq, Afghanistan and parts of Central Asia, and Pakistan. Later, Spain and Portugal were retaken by Christian Europe; and the Crusades made their mark upon Palestine by leaving a population of Christian immigrants.

Altogether, Muslim success was tremendous, convincing, and comprehensive. Not only did the armies succeed in battle, but a cultural transformation followed in their wake. Economic, political, and artistic greatness went with the new faith. The Muslims welded Arabian, Greek, Semitic, Persian, Egyptian, and Indian cultures into one vast civilization with Islamic law as a center. From Spain to India, Muslim faith provided a unity that tied various peoples and tongues to one book, to one claim of revelation, and to one law.

And the spread of the new faith continued. The Ottoman Turks, who took Byzantium (Istanbul) in 1453, established their own Islamic empire. They dominated the Middle East and the southern Balkans into the nineteenth century. Trade carried the faith down the east coast of Africa. And trade carried the faith also to Malaya, Indonesia, and China. India lived from the twelfth century until the eighteenth century with Muslim kings ruling in Delhi.

Confirmation of the faith, then, did appear for Muslims. It was a confirmation by successful conquest of peoples. But the sword carried with it a reordering of life which elicited individual and collective assent to a new social, political, and cultural order dictated by the Koran and its official interpreters. To many, Islamic truth is tied to its success as a rule for life. Islam, it is claimed, is establishing the kingdom of God on earth.

THE SHAPING OF MUSLIM THEOLOGY

The Koran lays down the fundamental religious ideas of Muslim faith. Central to these ideas is the oneness of Allah and the prophethood of Muhammad. But the Koran is not a book of theology. It is an unsystematic series of inspired utterances said to have been dictated to Muhammad. And the utterances direct themselves toward specific people during specific times.

As the religion spread rapidly through the Middle East and into Asia and North Africa, Muslims found it necessary to present a more precise statement of the faith. The Koran could be interpreted as saying many different things when read in different places and times. And some interpretations appeared to contradict other things stated in the text.

The preserved records of Muhammad's decisions, actions, and personal interpretations of his messages (*Hadith*) were helpful to those who interpreted the Koran. But *Hadith* itself seemed to grow and expand as new situations were encountered and as new teachers applied the Koran to new situations. Theology—the consistent ordering of principles for interpretation, application, and understanding of God's will—became a necessary preoccupation of Muslim thinkers.

Theology to many is a dreary, futile, and endless shuffling of terms concerning "that-ness" and "such-ness," "all-ness" and "not-ness." But for Muslims, the demand to do theology came as a series of questions that struck at the heart of the new order of thought about God and His rule on earth.

In the years following Muhammad's death, two major debates emerged among believers. These debates forced Muslims to begin to develop a theology. One debate concerned the doctrine of predestination. As stated in the Koran, predestination might negate free will and moral responsibility. The other had to do with the nature and consequences of sin. Interestingly, the questions were not posed initially by theologians. Instead, they emerged from clashes in Muslim society and government.

As we mentioned before, the leadership of the Arab Muslims went into the hands of the Ummayads, and the capital of the Sunni state was settled at Damascus. The rulers were accused by some to be living in self-indulgence, luxury, and waste inappropriate to submitters. With such charges against the Ummayad rulers, it seemed proper to some Muslims to oppose their rule.

To counter criticism, the rulers mounted an effort aimed at nullifying scrutiny into their moral lives. They employed a number of learned religious men to pull verses from the Koran which imply that everything happening in the world happens according to God's will (that is, God predestines all things). It would follow, these rulers insisted, that they ruled by God's will. To oppose them was to oppose God. And they showed the Koran was on their side.

The pious critics countered the rulers' arguments by adopting the polar position that man has the freedom to choose his actions and that he is responsible under God to choose what is right and good. They asserted that free will and moral responsibility are valid even though God is all-powerful.

Both sides in the argument had no trouble pulling from the Koran verses which seemed to support their point of view. The controversy made plain the need for a theology. Since the political order was tied to claims concerning who was Muhammad's successor, the debate required a theological resolution. The argument demanded the development of theological principles to clarify the relationship of God's sovereignty to man's moral responsibility. The underlying question was something like this: "What exactly does the Koran mean when it states that both predestination and free will are true?" and its corollary, "What theological principle might reconcile these two contrary assertions?"

A second debate emerged from the issue of sin and its consequences. In its simplest form the question posed was: "Is it possible to sin and yet remain a Muslim?" What is sin if it is possible to do it and yet remain a "submitter"? This too was an issue tied to social and political matters.

In the early years of the faith, one group took the position that true faith is indistinguishable from good works and obedience to the law. One is a true Muslim who acts like a Muslim, went the argument. Therefore all sin is rebellion. Rebellion is apostasy. And apostasy is punishable by death!

Again, the political undertones are clear. Rulers, particularly, thought it impossible or inconvenient to obey all of the laws of the faith to the letter. But if a rigid interpretation of sin as apostasy were taken, rulers who sinned should be overthrown by any means. It would be a pious act to assassinate a sinful ruler.

Another group argued that a distinction must be drawn between big sins and little sins. Big sins were those such as suggesting that God was not one but many (polytheism) or that the revelations given to Muhammad were lies. Big sins were unforgivable. Little sins, on the other hand, are forgiven by a merciful God. One is not to be excluded from the community of the faithful for committing little sins.

Still another group insisted that decisions concerning who is a true Muslim and who is not are matters only God can handle. Faith and works must be clearly separated. Faith is internal; it is not seen by other people. Only God can judge who is a true believer and who is false. No man dare judge another's faith.

Such issues as what constitutes sin, what constitutes status as a believer, and what infringements of the law are permissible drove Muslims to search for theological principles. They needed a rational order and consistency for the statements of the Koran. Rival religious ideas also contributed to the demand for theology. To define Muslim faith over against Zoroastrian, Buddhist, Christian, and Jewish faith forced Muslim thinkers to defend their claims and to find ways to show their faith a fulfillment of others. Military conquest might intimidate, but it did not necessarily convince.

Under such conditions, the theology that emerged from Muslim thinkers was apologetic (defensive) and legalistic. Legalism emerged first from the conviction among the orthodox that the Koran was the eternal revelation containing laws to be applied socially and politically. But legalism developed also as a rejection of other, more rationalistic means to assert and defend the faith.

In the eighth century a group called Mutazilites began to construct a rationalist theology. Committed to the rational procedures of Greek philosophy, they explored the implications of the Koran's statements about God, His unity, His justice, His power. Through their analysis they came to troubling conclusions concerning God, man, predestination, free will, and moral responsibility.

Mutazilite thinkers concluded that troubles over questions of free will, moral responsibility, big sins or little sins rested upon issues concerning the nature of Allah, His unity and His justice. Rational analysis of the Koran's statements concerning God's nature drove them to the conclusion that the divine nature is uncompounded (it is not made up of parts). But if God's nature is uncompounded, they concluded, the statements in the Koran about God's attributes—His wisdom, love, knowledge, power—could not be attributes (something other than God). They must be the same thing as God. Otherwise, it could be said that God was made up of parts.

The Mutazilite conclusion concerning God's logical unity implied that the Koran employed an imprecise and unsophisticated way of talking about God. This called into question the Koran's dictation by an angel. Does it follow that the angel was deficient in reason to make such imprecise statements? Or was the Koran not really dictated?

Mutazilite theologians used similar rigor when it came to talk about God's justice. If God judges men for their activities (as the Koran says), then men must be free to act. Otherwise, God is unjust. He could not justly condemn men for doing the things that they *must* do. The logic of moral discourse forces such a conclusion, they maintained.

Squaring Mutazilite conclusions about human freedom with statements in the Koran declaring God to be all-powerful and all-knowing remained a problem. Mutazilite thinkers chose to put limits upon God's power and knowledge in order to leave room for human freedom and moral responsibility.

Yet employing reason to develop a precise and consistent theology begged a more troubling question: If statements about God and His ways must conform to reason to be true, must God conform to reason in His acts? Must God be reasonable? And if so, is He *limited* by reason?

Orthodox Muslims thought the Mutazilites had gone too far in their thinking. Such rational speculation was rebellious and wrong. It went too far beyond the literal statements of the Koran. They opposed the Mutazilites, and they stamped out the movement by the tenth century.

But the Mutazilite speculation forced the orthodox camp to develop an alternative method for interpreting the Koran. The orthodox alternative to the use of reason and logic as the standard was "instrumental" reason. The orthodox did not reject rationality; but they chose to employ reason only as an instrument to extract from the Koran the ways in which its statements might be applied to specific situations. They employed reason as a tool to bolster and defend what was stated in the text.

Orthodox Muslim theologians, in effect, became legal experts. They were called *ulema,* meaning "those learned in religion." But the function of the *ulema* was to spell out the legal implications of the Koran and the *hadith.* They were not to extend the employment of reason to ask what ultimate rational principles such legal statements rested upon. From the ranks of the *ulema* came judges (*qadis*) and scholarly advisors (*muftis*). They issued definitive interpretations and applications of what the Koran prescribed as proper behavior. These thinkers were concerned with what people should *do,* not what people should *know.*

The result of such a method of theology is a curiously dialectical assertion of faith (a statement of belief marked by inner conflict). Thus, orthodox Muslims do not seek to resolve conflicting statements, but simply attempt to affirm both at once. An example appears in the orthodox conclusions concerning statements about God, His unity (oneness), and His attributes. The issue is set to rest by the orthodox with the assertion that God's attributes "are not He nor are they other than He." In sections where references are made to the "hands" of God or where He is said to "sit upon a throne," these hands and the sitting are not the hands and sitting of human beings. God is totally other than man. Yet it is not inappropriate to use human attributes to characterize God.

Regarding predestination, they assert that everything that happens results from God choosing it to happen. When a man acts, God creates in him the will, the power, the intention to act. Yet a man is responsible for what he does. God acts through a man, but a man acquires the responsibility for the act.

In these examples it is clear that reason is not employed as an independent standard to which any statement concerning God and His acts must conform. Reason is instead employed as an instrument to spell out the fundamental claims, even if they appear inconsistent to one another. Readers of the theological writings are reminded that the faithful are called to "submit" to the revelation of the Koran. The Koran holds the words of God.

Another alternative to rational theology also emerged. This alternative was the mystical movement of Sufism. The mystical alternative appealed to religious experience over against religious knowledge. Mankind must *experience* the reality of God, these claimed. Experience of God is not discursive knowledge; it is not information; nor is it the rational ordering of propositions. It is an encounter in which a person is overwhelmed by the reality of God.

Sufi thinkers chose to ignore the literal sense of the Koran. To them, the entire book is but an allegory of the soul's quest for God. Beyond and apart from the literal words lies a profound, mystical sense. The profound, mystical meaning is grasped when a person confronts God through an experience with Him.

Sufis employed their own curious circular argument to assert their case. If you know God, they insisted, you grasp the meaning of the scriptural statements. If you are puzzled by the scriptural statements, that shows you do not know God. Theological debate is relevant only to people who have not experienced God. To assert the significance of theological reasoning is to admit failure in the personal spiritual quest. Anyone who had intellectual problems with the Koran does not need to do more thinking. He needs to experience God.

Sufis became noteworthy and controversial for their development of techniques for experiencing God. And though they disavowed rationalism as a means by which to know more about God as enthusiastically as the orthodox did, their mysticism infuriated the orthodox. For Sufi mystics claimed that nature is infused with the presence of God to the point that God and nature cannot and should not be distinguished one from another. God is experienced as everywhere present, they argued.

Sufism did provide an alternative to the rational speculation of the Mutazilites. But the orthodox did not welcome Sufism. Orthodoxy requires that faith be tied to a literal reading of the Koran. Sufism survives only at the fringes of Islam.

THE MODERN SITUATION

When Columbus sailed to the New World, Islam was the largest of the world's religions. It had expanded to areas as far apart and as different from one another as Senegal, Central Asia, Indonesia, and the Philippines. Its geographical expanse was impressive. Equally impressive was the vigor with which it absorbed cultures scattered everywhere in the world.

Yet remarkable also was the speed with which the Muslim unity fell apart, leaving vast tracts of Africa and Asia caught in the net of an Islamic culture but without the political structure to make it what it claimed to be—namely, the rule of God on earth.

The first great blow to Islam's position was the decline of Arab dominance in the Middle East. The fall of Baghdad in A.D. 1258 marked the formal end of the Arab Empire. Mongols decimated Arab cities, killed untold numbers of the faithful, demolished cities, and then, strangely enough, converted to Islam.

So the faith survived the Mongol wave. And the Mongols, as the new champions of the faith (the Ottomans of Turkey and the Mughals of India) endured for a time, but never equaled the achievements of the Arab civilization.

By the eighteenth century, Muslim culture was disintegrating and fragmenting into various small empires. European powers surpassed Muslim countries economically and militarily. Muslims made no advances in science. And the arts caved in to a dispirited repetition of traditional themes. Deadness within and intrusions from without plagued Muslim societies from India through North Africa.

From the seventeenth century until the mid-twentieth century most Muslims lived under the rule of European colonial powers. Muslims lived under the guns of infidels. Yet the faith claimed to be the living witness of God's pattern for life on earth.

No contemporary appraisal of Islam should be made without carefully considering what it meant for Muslims to live in bondage to infidels. Among most Muslim peoples, efforts to throw off foreign rule were not successful until the mid-twentieth century. Even then, influences of Western procedures in law, administration, technology, and economics remained basic to the new independent nations. Great Britain, France, and the Netherlands have abandoned most of their colonies in India, North Africa, the Middle East, and Indonesia, but their customs remain.

When Muslims gained independence from European powers, many sought to establish new governments based upon the teachings of Islam. Pakistan, formed in 1947 when the British departed India, has made a sustained effort to work out the social and political implications of what it means to be a Muslim state while coexisting with non-Muslim nations. Many former colonies with a predominately Muslim population have chosen to identify themselves as Muslim nations, though they have found it necessary to compromise with European and American theories of political, economic, and judicial order.

The outstanding case of Muslim national resurgence in recent years is Iran. In a revolution that toppled the Shah Mohammed Reza Pahlavi and established the totalitarian theocracy of Ayatollah Khomeini, Iranians are attempting a return to traditional Muslim ideals of social order. Inspired by a man declaring himself the supreme interpreter of Allah's will, Iran revolted against the Shah (alleged to be an American puppet). The combination of fervent Islam and Persian nationalism, buoyed by billions of dollars in oil revenues, has helped the new religious state weather tremendous turmoil and violence in its first years.

The overthrow of the Shah resulted from a religiously inspired mass uprising of Iranian people. Thus, a frail and aged Shi'ite cleric living in exile forced the powerful Shah to abandon his throne and flee for his life.

Within weeks of the Ayatollah Khomeini's ascent to power, he initiated a reign of terror against supporters of the old order. The number of executions carried out by the new government is hard to estimate. Human-rights organizations in the West estimate the total at approximately 6000. Iranians themselves published a book with the names and photographs of nearly 8000 executed people. The actual number, including "street executions," is surely higher.

The executions were for theological crimes as well as political. The new regime does not discriminate between the two. Religious dissenters are classed with supporters of the old regime. At least 120 members of the Bahái faith (heretics in the eyes of Khomeini) have been killed for continuing to practice their religion. More have been imprisoned in an effort to make Iran a pure Islamic nation.

With the reign of terror has come a transformation in the daily lives of millions. Even the most secular among the Iranians have been forced to conform to a strict Islamic code of behavior.

The Islamic order does not admit a distinction between church and state, religion and government. Iran's 180,000 Mullahs have become agents of the state. Through tens of thousands of local mosques, they dispense food rations and fuel cards; issue business permits; censor books and plays; pass regulations; run the courts; collect taxes; recruit war volunteers; and issue interest-free loans to those considered deserving. The mosques also keep detailed records on every member of their congregations. These records provide a grass-roots intelligence file for the regime.

The Islamic Republic of Iran remains the only one of its kind. A few countries, such as Pakistan and the Sudan, have introduced versions of an Islamic code, but they have rejected any all-encompassing model of social order. And the much advertised exportation of the Khomeini revolution to other Muslim-populated nations has been a failure.

It remains an important question whether the Iranian Islamic state is a unique, fundamentally aberrant creation of one man or whether it is the natural consequence of applying the teachings of the Koran to modern life. To what extent is Iran a peculiar throwback to an earlier age?

One answer to the question lies with the fate of Islam in Iran after Khomeini. Provisions for a successor have been made by the

Ayatollah (he does not wish to make the mistake Muhammad made). Legally his successor must assume supreme political and religious control of an Islamic state. Yet it remains to be seen whether there is anyone waiting in the wings who is capable of filling Khomeini's turban.

It may be unfair to cite the Ayatollah's writings as representative of mainstream Muslim thought. His achievement is unique and special. Yet he claims to be spelling out the political implications of submission to God. And soldiers, students, and clerics display a zeal for his explanations of the Koran that require observers to give close attention to his words.

A major theme found in Khomeini's writing is a sharp criticism of Western life. Muslims, he says, have a duty to counter the way of life practiced in Europe and America. Emphasis upon comfort, commerce, wealth, and material goods have no place in a life dedicated to God. The subversion of Muslim nations began long ago when European colonists installed governments and then introduced laws and customs contrary to Islamic faith.

The toppling of the Shah's monarchy must be accompanied by a rejection of all non-Muslim practices which were a part of the Shah's program to "modernize" Iran. Drinking of alcohol, open adultery, Western cinema, night clubs, the liberation and employment of women outside the home, usury in the extension of commerce, advertisement of luxurious living, and an unequal distribution of wealth are all imported, sinful practices which must be outlawed. They are contrary to Islamic culture, Khomeini maintains.

In the place of the Western decadence, the Ayatollah advocates a return to the Koran as the standard of government and social life. The Koran contains provision for a complete social system, he maintains. Its law meets all of man's needs. Relationships within family, among neighbors, citizens, and other nations are all spelled out in proper terms by the Koran. Regulations regarding crime, property, industry, commerce, and agriculture are also a part of the Koran. Islam is a complete and comprehensive code for life. No situation in the world escapes the legal system contained in the pages of scripture, Khomeini insists.

We must emphasize again that the Ayatollah Khomeini does not speak for all Muslims. He is the product of a Shi'ite theological education. And he holds a great personal bitterness toward America and any nation that might have aided in moving Iran away from a literal application of the Koran to national life. His desire is also to push his nation toward greatness in the world. That greatness, in his eyes, is achieved not by industrial and scientific advances, but by conformity to the law of the Koran. Iran, he maintains, is building the rule of God on earth.

RECOMMENDED READING

Gibb, H.A.R. *Mohammedanism,* 2nd edition. Oxford University Press, 1953.

Hitti, Philip K. *Islam. A Way of Life.* Henry Regenery Company (by arrangement with the University of Minnesota), 1970.

Lewis, Bernard. *The Arabs in History.* Harper Torchbook, 1950.

Peters, F. E. *Children of Abraham.* Princeton University Press, 1982.

Smith, W. C. *Islam in Modern History.* Princeton University Press, 1957.

GLOSSARY

The terms defined below are central to discussions of Asian religious traditions. Additional terms are given further clarification in the body of the text.

Rendering Sanskrit, Chinese, or Arabic terms into our alphabet is a controversial task. For someone who reads any of these languages, no transcription of terms is adequate. For someone who does not know any of these languages, any system of transcription seems confusing. How to be accurate and precise without confusing those unfamiliar with Asian languages presents a problem. We have chosen a middle course here by providing conventional transcription methods with an additional rendering to aid pronunciation. Diacritical marks are kept to a minimum in the belief that only those necessary to aid pronunciation are helpful to the uninitiated.

Chinese terms are presented in the older Wade-Giles system of transcription. Pinyin appears in the body of the text in parentheses. The letter in brackets following the words below indicates its language, for example, **Yoga** [S]—i.e., a Sanskrit word. We will represent Arabic by [A], Chinese by [C], and Japanese by [J].

Advaita [S] (ud-vie-ta) The nondualist version of Hindu thought, associated primarily with the philosopher Shankara. It is nondual in its assertion that the essential reality of an individual person is identical with Brahman, the Absolute Reality. All selves are identical, for all are in essence one with the Absolute. Sometimes this view is called *Vedanta* because it is a dominant theme in the *Upanishad* literature (the end of the *Veda*).

Agni [S] (ug-nee) The god of fire in the *Veda* who carries the offerings of men to the skies. Sometimes Agni is referred to as the light within mankind.

Ahimsā [S] (uh-him-saa) A prominent concept in some sects of Hinduism and important to Buddhism. It involves a respect for all life to the point of practicing noninjury to any living thing. Gandhi gave the word new meaning in the advocacy of *Ahimsa* as "nonviolence" and as a technique for resistance to British rule in India.

Allah [A] (ull-aah) The name used by Muhammad for the Divine Being who reveals himself through the *Koran*. The term is thought to be related to the Hebrew *Elohim* and the Aramaic *Elah*.

Amitābha [S] (um-it-aab-ha) The celestial Buddha who created the Pure Land paradise of the West to which a faithful Buddhist retires as a waiting station upon death. The Pure Land School of Buddhism holds special interest in worship of *Amitabha*.

Anātta [S] (un-aat-uh) The Buddhist term for the doctrine of "No-self" or "No-ātman." Since the essence of a human is incapable of description, it cannot be said to exist in any conventional sense.

Arhat/Arhant [S] (ar-hut; ar-hunt) Literally the term refers to a "worthy one." This title is given to those Buddhist monks who attain liberation.

Asceticism The view that in order to attain perfection one must mortify the flesh by abstaining from anything bringing the body comfort or pleasure.

Ātman [S] (aat-mun) The Sanskrit term for the real self. In much Hindu thought it refers to the soul which is considered to be eternal and distinct from the ego, the sense faculties, or consciousness. The term is usually translated as the Soul or the Self.

Avalokiteshvara [S] (uv-a-lowk-it-esh-vara) The *Bodhisattva* who looks down on living beings with compassion. In Chinese Buddhism the figure is transformed into a female character called *Kwanyin*.

Avatāra [S] (uv-a-taar-a) The incarnation of God in some material form. *Avataras* are associated with *Vishnu* worship. Vishnu is thought to make periodic entrances into the world of matter—either as an animal or a human—in order to teach or to save.

Avidyā [S] (u-vid-yaa) Human ignorance, error.

Bodhisattva [S] (bowd-he-sutt-va) One who is destined to become a Buddha but who puts off enlightenment and liberation in order to help other living beings find the way to salvation.

Brahman [S] (brummun) In traditional Hindu thought it is the name for God, sometimes seen as a personal being, sometimes seen as nonpersonal. In its nonpersonal sense it is thought of as the ultimate power, the force that sustains the cosmos.

Brahmin [S] (brummin) The priestly class in Hindu religion and in the caste system. Generally it has held top status among the four castes. The word is related to Brahman.

Buddha [S] (bood-ha) An enlightened One, one who has gained realization. Siddhartha Gautama (563–483 B.C.) became a Buddha in the present age of the universe. Some later Buddhists maintain that there are heavenly Buddhas who are like gods. The chief of these is *Amitābha*.

Caste The social system of a stratified society which is to be traced to the *Veda*. Its origin probably lies in a combination of factors, including the old class system of the Aryan peoples, religious dif-ferences, craft guilds, and the assimilation of tribal groups into Hindu society. Beneath the regular castes are the "untoucha-bles"—those who are without social status and are considered unclean.

Ch'an [C] (chaan) The term literally means meditation and is used as the name for a type of Buddhist practice introduced to China from India. *Ch'an* is the Chinese equivalent for the Sanskrit word *Dhyāna*. The Japanese rendering of the term is *Zen*.

Confucius This is the Latinized rendering of the Chinese name K'ung Fu-Tzu, who lived from approximately 551–479 B.C. He is notable for reformulating the tradition expressed in the Chinese classics. His thought gave rise to a systematic ethic for the Chinese classics.

Dharma [S] (d-har-ma) Law, truth, or teaching. It is a term used to express the central teachings of Hindu or Buddhist religion. It implies that the essential truth about the way things are can be stated and that people should adjust to meet that norm.

Dhyāna [S] (dhyaana) The Sanskrit word for meditation. Various methods of meditation have been developed and are used by dif-ferent schools of religious practice in India. The word changes to *Ch'an* in Chinese and *Zen* in Japanese.

Dualism The theory that two independent and mutually irreducible elements comprise reality. These may be identified as mind and matter, as appearance and reality, or as good and evil, depending upon the specific dualist teaching being asserted.

Gautama [S] (gow-tum-ah) The name of the Buddha as transcribed from Sanskrit.

Guru [S] (goo-roo) A spiritual teacher who takes disciples. His au-thority is to be accepted implicitly by his pupils. And he takes responsibility for what his students do.

Hijra [A] (hidg-ra) Muhammad's move from Mecca to Medina in A.D. 622, taken as the base year for calculating the calendar of Muslims.

Hinayāna [S] (heen-ah-yaana) The lesser vehicle to salvation as dis-tinguished from the greater vehicle (*Mahāyāna*). It was originally a very negative term; members of the school prefer the term *Ther-avada*, "the teaching of the elders."

Imam [A] (im-aam) One who leads the congregation in the mosque.

Typically he is elected to do so by the community of the faithful. The title is also used by the *Shi'a* branch of Islam to refer to the leaders of the whole people under God who are awaiting the arrival of the "hidden Imam," a kind of Messiah.

Ishvara [S] (eesh-vara) The Lord, a term used by Hindus to refer to God in his personal manifestation.

Islam [A] (is-laam) Literally the term means submission to God (Allah). It is commonly used as the title of the faith preached by Muhammad.

Ismaili [A] (is-ma-eely) A group among *Shi'a* Muslims who elevate the role of the *Imam* to great significance.

Jati [S] (jaati) The Sanskrit word commonly translated as "caste."

Jihad [A] (ji-hud) The duty to engage in holy war if called upon to do so. It is one of the basic requirements of Muslim faith. Allah promises a heavenly reward to all who die in holy war.

Jinn [A] (djinn) An order of spirits in Muslim demonology.

Jivanmukti [S] (jeevan-mook-tea) Living release or liberation in Hindu faith. This is the state of a person who has attained *Moksha* or *Mukti* and is merely living out life, awaiting final liberation from rebirth.

Karma [S] (kar-ma) The law of cause and effect which determines one's status in life and in rebirth. No human act is without consequences, the law states.

Koan A problem which cannot be solved by ordinary discursive thinking or reasoning. It is used as a technique to break the hold of reason and to open a person to intuitive insight in Japanese Buddhism.

Krishna [S] The Blessed Lord of the text *Bhagavad Gītā* who advises Arjuna concerning the nature of reality and his place in it. Sometimes Krishna is referred to as an incarnation of Vishnu.

Kshatriya [S] (kshut-reeya) The warrior or military caste of traditional Hindu society. Generally it has been considered as second in rank to the priestly caste.

Mahātma [S] (muh-aatma) A title meaning "great soul" or "great man" often given to famous spiritual leaders of India.

Mahāyāna [S] (ma-haa-yaana) The Great Vehicle to salvation in Buddhism. This form of Buddhism which prevails in East Asia and derives its teaching from a "new explanation" of Buddha's teaching.

Mantra [S] (muntra) Holy words or verses in Hindu or Buddhist meditation techniques. A *mantra* is usually provided a pupil by a *guru* who holds insight into the specific needs of others.

Māyā [S] Illusion, deception, relativity of perception, or inaccurate insight are all connoted by this term. The *Upanishad* literature makes much of this term in arguing that the world of ordinary experience is false.

Moksha [S] (moe-ksha) Ultimate liberation or release from the round of existence in Hindu thought.

Monism The view that there is but one fundamental reality, and all else is derivative of that or the result of inaccurate insight or wrong thinking.

Muezzin [A] One who calls the faithful to pray in Islamic countries.

Muharram [A] (moo-hurrum) The name refers to the first lunar month of the Muslim year. The tenth of Muharram is sacred to *Shi'a* Muslims. It is a festival commemorating the death of Husain, the son of Ali. The location of his death, Karbala in Iraq, is a pilgrimage site.

Mukti [S] (mook-tea) An alternative Sanskrit term for liberation.

Nirvāna [S] (near-vaana) Literally a "blowing out" or a "cooling" of the fires of existence. It is the main word used in Buddhism for final release from the round of birth and death.

Pali (pa-li) The language into which Buddhist scriptures were first committed so far as is known today. The *Theravada* school holds to the Pali text. The language is associated with a north Indian dialect and relates to Sanskrit in much the way Italian relates to Latin.

Purāna [S] (pur-aanu) A text containing ancient Hindu stories. There are many of these texts, and they contain the lore associated with many gods and goddesses of the Hindu pantheon.

Sadhu [S] (sad-huu) A Hindu ascetic who is thought to hold special powers. He is given special privilege in Hindu society because he is one who has renounced the world.

Sāmkhya [S] An early Hindu system teaching that matter and spirit are separate and that the human spirit is in reality free, inactive, and an observer of matter.

Samsāra [S] (sum-saara) A term used in Hindu and Buddhist thought to describe the process of change in the universe, and in particular the round of birth and death to which mankind is subject.

Shaikh [A] (shy-ch) A prestigious person in general, but in Islam, a religious leader or head of a community. The *Sufi* sects take particular note of such a person.

Shaivism [S] (shy-vism) A Hindu sect devoted to the god Shiva as the lord who destroys and remakes the earth.

Shari'a [A] (shar-ee-ah) Islamic law.

Shi'a [A] (she-ah) The branch of Islam common to the more easterly regions, from Iraq through Iran into Pakistan. *Shi'a* Muslims trace their spiritual leadership back to Ali, the son-in-law of the prophet Muhammad.

Shirk [A] (sheerk) The Islamic term for idolatry, that is, holding to a view that there is a God beside Allah. This is a chief form of blasphemy to Muslims.

Shunyatā [S] (shoon-ya-taa) The emptiness which is the nature of all things, according to some schools of Buddhist thought.

Stupa [S] (stoopah) A burial mound for a Buddhist holy person which became formalized as a dome-shaped structure with elaborate gates and grounds. Lay people and monks walked around the structure to express reverence for the Buddhist ideal expressed in the life of the one honored. The pagoda and the dagoba (a shrine for sacred relics) in eastern regions of Buddhist influence are related.

Sunna [A] (soona) The traditional branch of Islam which is prevalent in Arab countries and in West and North Africa.

Sutra [S] (sootra) A sermon or saying of the Buddha. Literally it means a thread upon which a jewel is strung.

Tantrism A form of Hindu or Buddhist religion prevalent for a time in North India and Tibet which emphasized sacramental means toward enlightenment. Often the rituals required the breaking of caste rules and various taboos, including sex and diet.

Tao [C] (dow) A Chinese concept of the Way which is both a path of conduct and the principle governing the operations of the whole universe. Teachings about the Tao usually assert that one ought to live in harmony with nature's way, though there is considerable disagreement concerning what that way might be.

Theravāda [S] (tay-ra-vaada) Literally it means the "teaching of the elders." *Theravada* is the name usually given to the kind of Buddhism practiced in Sri Lanka and much of Southeast Asia. Its scriptures are written in the Pali language.

T'ien [C] (tyen) Chinese for heaven and also for God.

Tripitaka [S] (trip-it-aka) The Buddhist scripture. The term literally means "Three Baskets," and derives from a simile of passing along something to another in a container.

Upanishads [S] (oop-un-ish-ads) The last section of the Hindu scriptures, *Veda*. The texts making up this section discuss various aspects of ancient rituals and convey a complicated set of philosophical assertions concerning the human condition and the nature of reality.

Vaishnavism [S] (vie-shna-vism) A form of Hinduism dedicated to worship of the god, Vishnu. It has been heavily influenced by the thought of the philosopher Ramanuja.

Vedānta [S] (vay-daan-ta) The term literally means the end (or point) of the *Veda*. It usually refers to the teachings contained in the *Upanishads*.

Yoga [S] (yoe-ga) The general name for a body of practices in the Indian religious traditions involving both physical and mental disciplines. It is also used for a specific school of thought and practice within Hinduism. As a school it is closely tied to the teaching of *Sankhya*.

Zen [J] A type of Buddhist thought which has two branches. It is best known for its emphasis upon the experience of enlightenment as one which results from breaking down the commitment and attachment to the logical and rational ordering of experience.

A SELECT BIBLIOGRAPHY OF
MAJOR TEXTS

This bibliography lists some of the major texts of Asian religions. Texts of scriptural significance are listed first. Then we give major texts which stand alongside scripture to elaborate it or to add to its claims. Many books which might not carry "religious" significance in the West must be included among the sacred texts of Asia.

HINDU LITERATURE

SCRIPTURE: *Veda*—classified as *Shruti,* that is, "heard."

The texts were in a process of composition and compilation from ca. 1800–500 B.C. The texts fall into four categories: *Samhitas* (the earliest verses); *Brahmanas* (priestly writings/commentaries/rituals); *Aranyakas* ("forest texts"); *Upanishads* (speculative philosophical discourses). For each section there are numerous texts, each of which corresponds to one of the earliest, primary verses. Thus a schemata might be constructed to show the developing *Veda:*

Samhitas	Brahmanas	Aranyakas	Upanishads
Rigveda Samaveda	Aitareya Pancavimsha	Airetya	Aitreya
Yajurveda	Chandogya Taittiriya	Taittiriya	Chandogya Taittiriya
	Shatapatha	Brihad	Brihadaranyaka
Atharvaveda	Gopatha Mundaka		Prashna Mandukya

The chart provides only a rough indication of the structure of the *Veda*. There are many more individual texts which fall under the categories of *Samhitas, Brahmanas, Aranyakas,* and *Upanishads.*

NONSCRIPTURAL LITERATURE: *Smriti*: "remembered."

Sutras

Sutras (literally "threads") were written from about 500–200 B.C. These writings are designed to present (actually re-present) the requirements of *Vedic* religion. Most consist of brief maxims which are difficult to grasp without the aid of a teacher or commentator with knowledge of the *Veda*. There are various sorts of *Sutra* texts: *Srauta* (priestly); *Grihya* (domestic rituals); *Dharma* (social duties); and a host of *sutras* dealing with grammar, logic, vocabulary, etc.

The best known *Sutra* text is called *Vedanta Sutra*. It is a synopsis of the *Upanishad* literature. It presents the major insights of the *Upanishads* (for the purpose of clearing up controversies concerning meaning). Nearly every great thinker of Hindu religion has written a commentary explaining the *Vedanta Sutra*.

Epic Literature

India boasts two epic poems of considerable significance to Hindu religion. The *Mahabharata* is a long poem comparable to Homeric epic literature in the sense that it presents the legendary origins and struggles of a whole people. The *Mahabharata* is considerably longer than any other epic poem of world literature (some 90,000 stanzas). An important section of the text is known as *Bhagavad Gita*.

The second epic, *Ramayana,* differs in content and style. It claims a single author, Valmiki. It is the story of the kidnapping, rescue, and testing of Prince Rama's devoted wife, Sita.

Puranas

The *Puranas* (ca. 300 A.D. and on) present ancient lore concerning gods, goddesses, wise men, teachers, and the auspicious actions of heroic figures. One of the most significant is the *Bhagavata Purana,* dedicated to the glorification of the god, Vishnu. It tells the story of Vishnu's incarnation as Krishna, developing the Krishna legend in terms of his youthful years prior to the battle scene of the *Bhagavad Gita.*

BUDDHIST LITERATURE

SCRIPTURE: *Tripitaka* (Sanskrit); *Tipitaka* (Pali).

There are three sections made of three distinct types of texts. *Vinaya* deals with the disciplinary regulations for the community of monks. *Sutra* relates discourses of the Buddha. *Abhidharma* is a set of texts giving detailed discussions of matters spoken of in earlier sections. Sections of the scriptures often appear as individual publications, for example, the *Dhammapada* or the *Lankavatara Sutra*.

The canon of scripture used by the *Theravada* Buddhists (called "Pali Canon") was closed by the first century B.C. Buddhist texts continued to appear which were included in the *Mahayana* Buddhist canon. It is doubtful that the *Mahayana* canon was ever closed; no concensus could be reached across the vast geographical areas *Mahayana* covered. Let us look at the major texts considered canonical by *Mahayana* Buddhists.

The *Prajnaparamita-Sutra* ("Sutra on the Greater Wisdom") exists in several versions of various lengths. It marks a new emphasis upon the *Bodhisattva* and the ideal of compassion at the same time as it speaks of the emptiness of existence (*Shunyata*). It is *Sutra* literature in the sense that the sayings are attributed to the Buddha.

The *Saddharmapundarika-Sutra* ("Sutra on the Lotus of the True Teaching") attempts to combat the conservative doctrines of the *Theravada*, primarily by characterizing them as shallow and selfish in their pursuit of enlightenment.

The *Sukhavativyuha-Sutra* ("Sutra on the Pure Land") argues the case for devotion to the Buddha as a means to salvation, which is characterized as a paradise.

The *Avatamsaka-Sutra* ("Flower-ornament Sutra") gives an extensive portrayal of the Bodhisattva's serach for enlightenment. It views existence as interdependence of impermanent elements.

Numerous sutras teach the existence of the Buddha *Amitabha* ("Infinite Light") and his paradise in Western space, together with doctrines of devotion and faith as means for rebirth in paradise.

There appeared various attempts to summarize the essence of *Sutra* literature. Two main *Sutras* of this type are *Vajracchedika-Prajnaparamita-Sutra* ("Diamond Sutra") and the *Hrdaya-Prajnaparamita-Sutra* ("Heart Sutra").

TALES.

Numerous tales of significance for moral ideas concerning life appear in a collection called *Jataka,* the birth stories and accounts of
Buddha's previous lives.

COMMENTARIES.

Commentaries on all texts appear in Sanskrit, Tibetan, Chinese,
Japanese, and Korean, together with translations and additions to
canonical texts. Buddhist studies generally require some familiarity
with Sanskrit, Chinese, and Japanese. Yet those languages provide
access to only the extended teachings of the *Mahayana*. Countries of
Southeast Asia, most of which hold to the Pali Canon, hold texts in
the languages of Burma, Thailand, Kampuchea, Vietnam, Malaysia
and Indonesia.

CHINESE LITERATURE

CONFUCIAN TEXTS

Confucius was concerned to point out the proper order of life as
it existed in the Golden Age of the early dynasties. To do so he pointed
to the Classics. These, together with four other books, comprise the
Confucian scripture.

THE CLASSICS

All of these purport to date from pre-Confucian times and to
represent the earliest literature of China. Modern scholarship disputes the claim. But the Confucian school saw itself as the protector
and transmitter of this ancient literature. These five books became
the chief object of study for the educated class of China for a couple
thousand years. They are held by Confucianists to contain not only
the answers to all the most important questions about history, but
also the embodiment of moral law.

I Ching ("The Book of Change") is a book of divination which
originally made sense out of the cracks which appear on a tortoise
shell when heated. Eventually *yarow* sticks made to fall in a particular
way are read in terms of patterns designated by the book. The assumption is that change in the world occurs according to patterns,

and the patterns of change can be known so that people can adjust their lives accordingly.

Shu Ching ("The Book of History") is a collection of ancient Chinese chronicles recording monarchs and their accomplishments. Interspersed with the accounts, however, are passages of moral counsel and advice. Contained in the *Shu Ching* is a reference to the Mandate of Heaven and its removal or transfer to the most worthy.

Shih Ching ("The Book of Odes") contains folk songs and poems probably used at ceremonies performed by kings and officials.

Li Chi ("The Book of Rituals") contains the rules for conduct of every day life. Implied is the notion that obligation must be acted out in terms of formal behavior.

Ch'un-ch'iu ("The Book of Spring and Autumn Annals") provides brief and obscure records of events affecting the state of Lu, Confucius' home area.

THE ADDITIONAL FOUR TEXTS

Lin-yu ("The Analects") is a collection of the sayings of Confucius and provides the most comprehensive account of his teaching, even though it seems to lack a clear arrangement. No precise date can be assigned to the work. It was probably compiled by disciples after Confucius' death.

Tao Hsio ("The Great Learning") is a capsule summary of the teachings of Confucius.

Chung Yung ("The Golden Mean") is traditionally ascribed to a grandson of Confucius. Its central emphasis is on the Middle Way or moderacy as the highest ideal of conduct.

Hsiao Ching ("The Classic of Filial Piety") is a prime scripture. It bases the sense of moral obligation upon respect for parents and obligation to ancestors.

One other major text must be included in any list of Confucian texts. It is *Meng Tzu* ("The Book of Mencius"). Living in the fourth century B.C., Mencius became Confucius' chief interpreter for Chinese history. He developed a theory of morality and of benevolent government which served as the ideal for centuries.

THE TAOIST TEXTS

Tao Te Ching ("The Book of the Way and Its Power") is attributed to Lao-Tzu. This is a small book of some five thousand characters divided into eighty-one chapters. It counsels avoidance of material gain, refusal to identify happiness with the acquisition of particular things, and the eschewing of ambition. Letting things operate according to their inner way allows all things to simply be and to do what they are made to be and to do.

Chuang Tzu ("The Book of Chuang-Tzu) is named after a philosopher who lived some two centuries after Lao-Tzu, and he is reported to have died around 270 B.C. Philosophical Taoism traces itself primarily to the writings of Chuang-Tzu. Yet his writing is loaded with irony, paradox and humor. A major theme in his writing is the distinction between what is natural and what is artificial (human creation).

MUSLIM LITERATURE

Koran ("The Recitation") is the collected revelation given to Muhammad by the angel Gabriel over a period of some twenty years. The book is divided in 114 chapters called *surahs*. The arrangement puts the longer revelations first (though they were the last ones received) and the shorter ones last.

Hadith ("Report") is a report purporting to transmit the words and deeds of Muhammad. It is not scripture, but since it provides information concerning Muhammad's application of the *Koran* to various situations, it ranks high as an aid to interpreting scripture.

Al Tafsir ("The Exegesis" of Al-Tabari) is a tenth centruy A.D. document and the foremost exegetical text of the *Koran*. It combines legal, historical, and philological commentary of great density by tracing its interpretations back to the contemporaries of Muhammad, the Companions.